Becoming

Unique & Unstoppable

**Courageous Journeys of Real Women
Daring to Believe!**

Creative Force Press

Becoming Unique & Unstoppable © 2013 by the Unique & Unstoppable™ Team

Published by Creative Force Press
4704 Pacific Ave, Suite C, Lacey, WA 98503
www.CreativeForcePress.com

All rights reserved. No part of this publication may be reproduced, stored in a retrieval system, or transmitted in any form or by any means--for example, electronic, photocopy, recording--without the prior written permission of the publisher. The only exception is brief quotations in printed reviews.

ISBN: 978-1-939989-00-0

Library of Congress Cataloging-in-Publication Data is on file at the Library of Congress, Washington, DC.

"Unique & Unstoppable™" is a copyrighted ministry name for the women's ministry of Capital Christian Center, Olympia, WA. The stories contained in this book are true, based on the individual views and personal testimonies of each contributor.

www.Go2CCC.org
www.UniqueAndUnstoppable.com

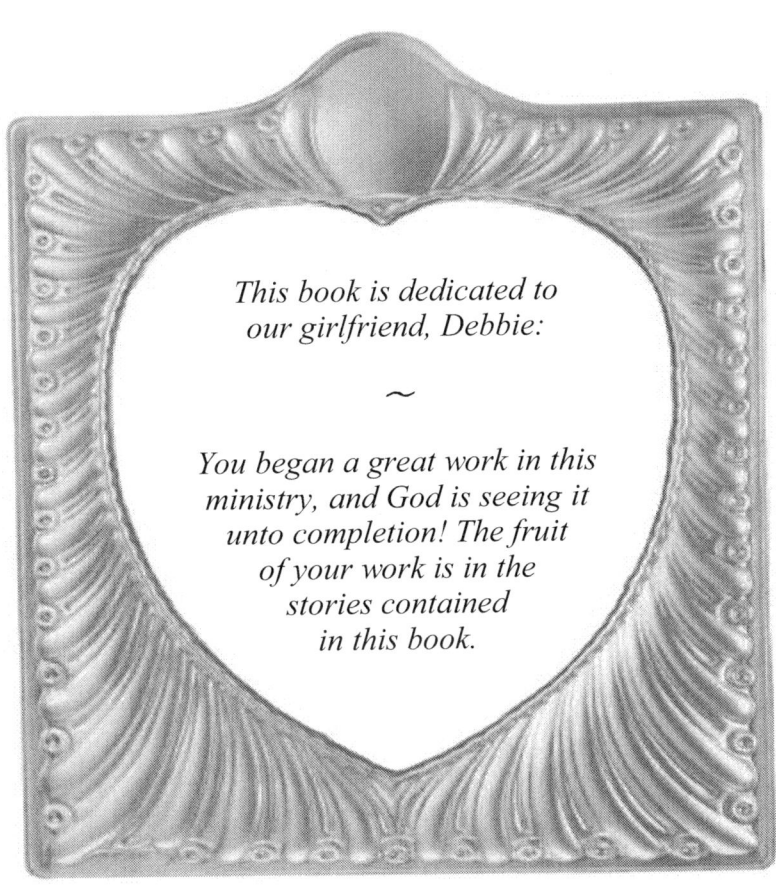

This book is dedicated to our girlfriend, Debbie:

~

You began a great work in this ministry, and God is seeing it unto completion! The fruit of your work is in the stories contained in this book.

Contents

Foreword...	7
Introduction..	9
Change is a Choice - Cortnei Boyd...............................	11
Redeeming the Scars - Crystal Wade...........................	15
We, Not Me...Doing Life Together - Rhea Hernandez...........	21
Regaining Confidence - Valerie Avington......................	25
Restoring God's Original - Trisha Ferguson...................	29
The Beach - Christina Sipe......................................	33
Letting Go of Timidity & Letting God be Big - Krista Dunk.......	37
When Leaders Lose Their Way - Danielle Payment...............	41
Abused, Abandoned, Adored! - Tammy Redmon...................	45
Not Even a Hint of Smoke - Sherry Elliott.......................	51
From Brokenness, to Healed & Unstoppable - Melissa Wade...	57
Dancing in Freedom - Carla Baptiste..............................	61
I am Chosen - Darci Coyne..	65
The Kaleidoscope Effect - Deborah McLain......................	71
Limitless - Kimm Bryant..	77
Answers & Acceptance from God - Sheila Simms................	81
Overcoming Addiction, Embracing Purpose - Sharma Drake....	85
Created to Be Me - Peggy Barry..................................	89
Strength & Courage Under Fire - Colette Jensen................	95
From Nothing to Everything - Reva Brown......................	99
Restored to Joy - Margaret Stratham............................	103
Believe to Receive - Ruth Wade.................................	107
A Foundation of Faith - Dorothy Haase.........................	111
Love Check - Alyssa Hamilton...................................	115
Salvation Prayer..	122
Contributors..	123

Foreword

One of the most exciting things for me in my life is hearing the stories of God's grace and favor in other people's lives. When I first became a Christ follower, it was my heart's desire to see people walking in His goodness. I experienced such a transformation in my own life, I wanted to share with everyone who would listen.

Today, I am the pastor of Capital Christian Center, where I get to hear stories of hope, healing and transformation in people's lives all the time. People who choose to be unique and unstoppable, and who declare their trust in God, are allowing Him to be the author and finisher of their life story.

The dictionary defines *unique* as having no like or equal; unparalleled, incomparable, not typical, unusual. Being *unstoppable* is not being capable of being stopped or surpassed; unbeatable, forceful.

The stories in this book are of women who have faced real-life challenges, but chose to be unstoppable. I love stories like this, because all of us can gain wisdom from their life lessons and how they put their trust in God.

I want to encourage you today: get ready to gain wisdom for the things that you are facing. I believe these stories are going to inspire *you* to be unique and unstoppable!

Dave Minton
Senior Pastor, Capital Christian Center

Introduction

Matthew 28:19 says to gather in the unchurched and disciple them into devoted followers of Christ. Unique & Unstoppable is a women's ministry that lives out that calling by encouraging women to *become* unique and unstoppable. We are excited to celebrate all women who have received Christ, have been transformed by His love, and who reflect Him in their own unique and unstoppable ways.

We wrote this book to celebrate the uniqueness of women and encourage them to live unstoppable lives because they have a Father who celebrates who they are, and He has given them power to live blessed, boundless lives.

The true stories in this book are told by real women; women who dared to believe that God could change their circumstances, hurts, perspectives, and hearts. We hope this book will encourage women to embrace and celebrate their uniqueness, the uniqueness God has given them, and realize that with God they have an unstoppable force living on the inside of them to do great things for HIM!

Danielle Payment
Women's Pastor, Capital Christian Center

Cortnei Boyd - Change is a Choice

"And above all things have fervent love for one another, for 'love will cover a multitude of sins.'"

1 Peter 4:8

Chapter 1

I started attending church when I was 12. I wasn't raised in a Christian home. I knew about God and believed in God, but that's where it started and stopped. My parents divorced when I was nine years old, and from then on, my dad and I had a pretty shaky relationship. Looking back now, I realize he did his best, especially in the midst of his own pain, but at the time, that didn't change how it made me feel. During the divorce and after, I took my mom's side and saw my dad as the bad guy. In my eyes, he didn't take care of us like he should have and he cared more about himself and getting back at my mom than he did about taking care of his children. I felt extremely rejected and angry.

As a result, I didn't know what a happy, healthy, successful marriage looked like. Marriage was something that I wanted no part of…ever. Throughout my childhood and early teen years, I strongly believed that I was not going to get married and was not going to have kids. I was going to be a strong, independent woman. I didn't need a man. Why would I want to get married if it would just end in a divorce? Why would I want to have children and make them go through what I went through?

Then I met Evan. I had seen him around at church youth group and always thought he was attractive, but that was about it. One night when I was 16, he was singing during praise and worship and God told me that I was going to marry him. It wasn't an audible voice or anything, but I knew it was God. A thought like that was so far from anything I would ever think! I became anxious and nervous and my mind was conflicted. What was I supposed to think? What was I supposed to do? I certainly wasn't going to tell anyone. I tried to blow off the thought, "God didn't really mean that or say that," but it would not go away. It was the first time I remember God really talking to me, and it was so different than any experience I had ever had.

After that, all my beliefs about marriage and my life changed. We dated for three years and got married when I was nineteen. He is the single greatest blessing God has ever given me. The Lord has used him to bring so much healing to my life. He has taught me real love, forgiveness, patience and pretty much every good quality a person can possess. He is my crown, the thing I am most proud of in my life.

Newly married, I was also hungry for more of God and wanted to grow in my faith. I spent about a year working with a small team at our church, leading the youth in worship. I noticed the wisdom and love for God that my leader had, and I wanted that too. I asked her if I could serve with her on the women's leadership team, and that is when everything changed.

Serving with the women's team opened my eyes to such a wealth of wisdom that I had never experienced before. I was exposed to a spiritual depth that I desperately wanted and my new friends made it seem attainable. I felt confident that *I could have* what they had. Up until that point, I was under the impression that I was too young, too immature, too "whatever" to have the relationship with God that I wanted. Being part of a group of strong, Godly women gave me a new level of faith. The women on the team valued my opinion, poured into my life and believed in me. I have been open to what they say and the direction they lovingly give me, but they always send me back to God to find out His will for my life.

This journey has not been easy. When I surrounded myself with wisdom so far beyond what was ever modeled to me, I was challenged. When I thought I was doing things right because I was just doing what I knew, I would get told or shown that it wasn't really God's right way. So, I've had to make choices. Many times I've had to lay down my pride or push away fears and obey what God was showing me, either through the wisdom of others or from my quiet time with Him.

Change is always a choice. No one forced me to change or grow - I chose to. I pruned many things and people out of my life - anything that was holding me back from where God wanted to take me - and it was hard. I also had to change my attitude a lot! It was almost always my internal thinking and reactions, things like, "Did she really just say that to me? There is no way I will listen to that," or "They are so wrong, they don't know anything about me." Regardless of whether my feelings were justified or not, there was always something God wanted to show me. Whenever a nerve was hit, I could either let my heart grow hard in that area or with that person, or I could let God deal with what he wanted to deal with in me. Had I not been open to wisdom and God's direction, I would not be where I am today.

These women have absolutely changed my life. I cannot stress enough the importance of seeking Godly council and wisdom. There were times when I was clueless about how to ask God for help in my marriage or pray and believe for things I needed. There were times of confusion about what God thought of me or how much He loved me. These women taught me all of those things. They taught me how to go to God's Word, showed me how to pray, talked about their own challenges and what they did to overcome them, and modeled to me what walking with God looked like.

I always knew that I was created for a purpose and that my life was going to make a difference in the world. But it wasn't until I realized that no one can live out *my* purpose but *me*, that I really started to change. God can give us all the direction and surround us with all the wisdom that we need, but to make a difference in His Kingdom, it takes our obedience and submission to that wisdom, paired with taking action, to truly change.

Questions:

1. Do you surround yourself with women who have Godly counsel and wisdom?
2. What are the hard changes needed in your life, and are you willing to make these changes?
3. Will you seek the Lord for what women you could surround yourself with for the rest of this year?

Crystal Wade – Redeeming the Scars

"Yes, I have loved you with an everlasting love; therefore with loving kindness I have drawn you. Again I will build you, and you shall be rebuilt."

Jeremiah 31:3-4

Chapter 2

I have a scar: two actually, one on my left inner-arm just above my elbow and another on my left foot covering a good part of my ankle. I have had them for as long as I can remember. When I was younger, I would sometimes ask my mom about how they came to be. She would tell me of the time when at only three months of age, I caught a bad case of whooping cough, was rushed by helicopter to a private hospital and nearly died. I liked the helicopter part, but I was always mesmerized when she would tell me of just how close to death I came, and how the doctors were preparing her and my dad for my passing. Because my lungs had filled up with fluid, it was hard for me to breathe and the only way they could get liquids to my body was through sticking IVs in my foot and arm. I sometimes think of that story and how easy it would have been for me at such a young age, with no ability to fight for myself, to slip into death. But somehow God decided to intervene, and the circumstances surrounding my survival leave no doubt that it was only through His intervention that I was kept alive.

I love my scars. I love that they remind me of God's intervention in my life as a baby. They are symbols of His mark on me, and in some ways, I am proud of them. They remind me that I was set apart for Him to accomplish His purposes in the life He has given me.

There have been many more scars along the way. They may not have left physical marks but the ones beneath the surface, on the heart, have had the most lasting effects. When I think about my greatest scars, they have often been tied to my greatest blessing – my family. I was three years old when my parents divorced and my mom married my step-dad. Being later adopted and raised by him, I was from a young age blessed to have two great dads, one amazing mother, step parents, siblings, and a family who lovingly raised me as their own. I have truly never known, in an earthly sense, any greater unconditional love than the love of my family. I am convinced it is because of their love that I was able to receive God's love in my life at a young age. But, like any family, we have had our battles, our wounds, and they have left their scars.

At 15, my parents divorced and, in my young adolescent mind, my life seemed to fall apart. It was a gradual process, but the wounds went deep because the only foundation I had ever known felt like it fractured into a million pieces. I was left with an incredible void and a handful of pieces of my life that I knew I had no ability to make whole again.

After the divorce, I was left with the indelible impression that my father had abandoned the family, and most certainly, had abandoned me. Up to this point, we had been very close. Having adopted and raised me, I cherished the fact that my father didn't just love me because he had to. He loved me because he chose to. This all came to a halt as my parents struggled to mend the brokenness of their own hearts and deal with the ramifications of a separated family. At the time, I didn't understand why my father had moved away and had, to me, moved on. I also didn't understand why he had left me. There were times while he was still there that I felt his absence. That hurt. During a time in my life when I needed my father more than ever, I felt robbed, abandoned, and emptiness filled my heart. The security of my father's love was no more, and I was left with a sense of being damaged, even if I didn't know to what extent.

Perhaps the greatest effect was to my identity, and how I viewed my own value and worth. After all, I reasoned, if my father didn't want me what did that say about me? There must be something wrong with me. This mindset affected many areas of my life including my eating habits, extracurricular activities, and especially my view of men and romantic relationships. And while it was certainly a temptation for me to fill the void left by my father with other men, I decided to do the opposite. Unknowingly, I erected walls in my heart that would protect me from facing the excruciating rejection from men I had felt with my father. I'd be an independent, strong woman, and after all, I had God – I didn't need a man, right?

But the longing in my heart for male attention would persist, and in some seasons have reduced me to a puddle of tears at a moment's notice. Always lurking in the back of my mind was that I was unworthy of love. There were so many times in high school and college I would see a couple, or perhaps a father and daughter, and I would feel an ache in my heart. During those times, I never felt more alone, overlooked, and ignored which would only re-affirm the view I had of myself as inadequate and unworthy.

I am thankful for my family and church community during those seasons. If it hadn't been for them, I'm sure I would have made some very poor decisions in my vulnerability.

Thankfully, I serve a God who didn't leave me in my brokenness. When I finally let God into those places of pain in my heart, deep healing began. And I also realized that God could not heal what I kept in the dark and refused to admit.

I was being set free; free to scale the walls I had so efficiently erected to protect myself. I finally came to a place of complete surrender to God. I placed my trust in Him to expose the lies I had internalized for so long. "You are not worthy." "You are not good enough." "You are inadequate." God began to break through all of it and I started believing that I *am* beautiful, worthy and desirable.

During this process, God also began to give me a whole new grace and forgiveness for my father. God restored our relationship, and it's no longer marred by pain, misunderstanding, and disappointment. Last Christmas, my father gave me the greatest gift. He told me something I will never forget. When I was a student, he would sometimes make trips to my campus in the hopes of finding me. I never knew it. He would come into my dorm or walk around the area hoping that I would come out so he could see me. He had done this numerous times throughout my life. He said that he always loved me and always wanted me, but had been unable to communicate or express it. To say I was surprised was an understatement. Perhaps more than anything, I was in awe of my God. I was amazed that my Heavenly Father would take such a sensitive area of my life, those times when I felt most alone, abandoned, and forgotten, and reveal to me that he had been there all along. I wasn't overlooked or ignored. I was desired and wanted.

God took my shameful, hurtful experiences and rewrote my story. He took my scars and turned them into beautiful stories of redemption and grace. I am set free from the lies of the enemy, and I have come to a whole new understanding of the character of my Heavenly Father. Now I can look at my scars and proudly show them to others. This is my story of *grace*.

Questions:

1. Can you think of a time when God had intervened in your life?
2. What scars have been left on your heart?
3. Will you allow God to take your scars and turn them into beautiful stories of redemption and grace?

Rhea Hernandez - We, Not Me... Doing Life Together

"But seek first the kingdom of God and His righteousness, and all these things shall be added to you."

Matthew 6:33

Chapter 3

I've always been a dreamer. I've always made plans to accomplish my dreams, and I've always wanted to be more than I thought I could be.

Throughout my childhood, I often wondered where I fit in. I tried everything to be wanted and accepted. As a young girl I was chubby with frizzy, naturally curly hair and went on my first diet in the fifth grade. I was accident-prone, with a new broken bone about every other year. I felt inside exactly like the image you are beginning to get as you read my words.

I never felt chosen so I would compete to be chosen. Everything in life became a competition for me: competing for friends, family, life, and love. I wanted to be everyone's first choice. I competed for a place in my family, so I would feel more valuable. Despite having a loving family and friends, this self-concept grabbed hold of me.

My parents and I had a great relationship, until age ten, when my mom and I began struggling in our relationship. I became rebellious and started looking elsewhere for acceptance. I wanted to have a great relationship with my mom, but the hormones, independence and my deep need for acceptance got in the way. In high school, I started finding temporary love from men, but soon found myself empty and alone on the inside again. I was going nowhere fast.

At age 20, I gave my life to Jesus: a man who would love me for me. He chose me, and I didn't have to do anything to make Him choose me. I felt assured of His love and acceptance and nothing I could ever do would change that. From that moment, my life changed, and God gave me a hope and a future that I was ready for.

God began mending the broken areas of my life, but I continued struggling with acceptance and fulfillment. Over the next two years, God was digging out the junk in my life, and began settling His everlasting love and acceptance within my heart. I began growing in my relationship with the Lord, and He was my everything. He literally became the air I breathed. I became content and in love with God!

Then I met Steve. He became my best friend and showed me what it was like to be loved simply for who I was. I wasn't used to the kind of guy that just wanted to get to know me and treat me well…you know what I'm talking about. At times, I felt like it was too good to be true and almost sabotaged it, until I realized it was God and just accepted His gift.

Steve and I got married the following year, but I was a little blinded by love. In my idealistic mind, marriage was supposed to have the cute little house, the white picket fence and the well-behaved children playing outside. I was the princess and my prince would serve me! This silly fairy tale was etched in my mind. I soon learned that having a successful marriage would require me to give, and then give some more, to serve, and serve some more. I also learned that communication, in forms other than yelling and demanding, was vital. God had more work to do in me.

My mom and I may have had some differences along the way, but she taught me to be a strong woman and speak my mind, to fight for what I wanted in life, to take no "guff" from anyone, and to stand up for myself. These are valuable, except I took these same principles into my marriage and spoke my mind at all the wrong times. We had power-struggle tug-o'-wars through the first seven years of marriage, neither of us wanting to give in. My competitive spirit still wasn't submitted to our relationship.

I never wanted Steve to show me up in any area, including ministry. We began serving God and His house as youth pastors. Life and the busy-ness of helping others became top priority in our family. It came at a price: our marriage was hurting. Steve and I worked hard to achieve everything we wanted in ministry. God had given me a picture of the dreams and plans He had in store, and I had always kept that in my heart. The emotional pull to be the wife and mother my family needed from me versus the dreams God had placed in my life *seemed* to be in competition with one another. I wanted so badly to be in full time ministry and to make it my career, but the financial struggle and the need to be at home with my children all competed for a place. I was often upset that Steve would get to have that place in ministry and not me. When would it be *my* turn to be all He created *me* to be? Our marriage was hurting, yet I wanted nothing more than to be all He wanted *me* to be! I forgot that *me* and *he* had to become *we*!

It took a lot of humility to learn how to be God's daughter and to be content in that. Becoming submissive to God in being the wife and mother my husband and children needed has been a continuous work of submission, humility, patience, love, and commitment. I'm so grateful for His work in my life. Now I find myself walking in my calling. I am first a daughter of the King, second a wife and third a mother – it's funny that this priority list was so hard for me to understand. I tried to skip ahead of the stepping stones needed to get me to where He wanted me.

Last year I started accepting my husband as the pace-setter for our lives, and lined myself up with the vision for our lives *together*. As we approach our ten-year anniversary, I am glad we've never settled for second best during our trials. Steve has taught me that good really is the enemy of great. He's right, and because of that, we are living a full life today.

God has given me a new perspective of submission, and what it means to live a life fulfilled. No longer are my ways higher than His ways, but *His* ways and *His* thoughts are higher than mine. (Isaiah 55:8-9). I am getting set free by applying that principle in every area of life.

I am thankful to finally be in a place where I can see God's promises happening. He said that as we submit our ways to God, He gives us the desires of our hearts. And I have seen that to be true. Dreams that have been in my heart for twelve years are now coming to pass, and I have found myself ministering to others in unexpected ways. I thank God for His grace that has carried us through. He has plans for our family. It's not about me and *my* dreams, but about *our* dreams and the plans He has for us *together*. Together, we are unstoppable.

Questions:

1. Have you ever wondered where you fit in and tried to make a place for yourself with your own strength?
2. When have you not felt accepted in the past?
3. Will you allow the *Lord* to give you the acceptance that is needed in your life?

Valerie Avington - Regaining Confidence

"And to not be conformed to this world, but be transformed by the renewing of your mind, that you may prove what is that good and acceptable and perfect will of God."

Romans 12:2

Chapter 4

As a child I always felt strong, and I was okay with me. One early childhood memory was when my mother was pregnant with my younger brother and we were stopped at a red light. I remember my mom turning to me and saying in a very calm and steady voice, "Valerie, I need for you to get out the car and get something." I calmly responded back, "Okay." She added, "I cannot take my foot off the brake, and I need you to go get the catalytic converter that just fell out the bottom of the car." I did! I walked up the hill and saw the long, steel piece of machinery my mother was talking about. I was six years old. There was no fear, no worry, and no doubt that I could do what was requested of me! I was told later that it was really heavy, but I picked it up with no hesitation and no strain, and brought it back to the car.

I was always fearless as a young person. I was blessed to grow up in God's house and to hear and believe the message that I was destined for greatness.

As a teen, in the midst of challenges, mistakes and stupidity, I still felt God's presence in and around my life. I had made some bad choices including being impure before marriage, smoking and even selling drugs. I had lost my childlike confidence and obedience. But even during those times, God was near.

As an adult with four young children, my husband and I separated for a year. When we decided to reconcile, we rededicated our lives to Christ and decided as a family to live according to God's standard. This would take courage and a lot of faith, but it was the best decision we ever made.

I often think back on the strength and confidence I walked in as a child, and how life's experiences and bad decisions brought me to a place of questioning, hesitation, fear, and disobedience with God. When my mom instructed me to pick up that heavy car part so long ago, she was telling me, "I trust you, you can do this, I need you," and I simply believed her.

Recently, I have been stepping back into that childlike confidence; that no-doubt, no-hesitation, fearless response to my Heavenly Father. Hebrews 13:8 says, "Jesus Christ is the same yesterday, today and forever." That means the same strength and confidence that overshadowed me at age six is still available to me today. And though at one point my bad choices and decisions stole my confidence, God restored me. As a child, I didn't have to prove anything. Matthew 18:3 says this: "Verily I say unto you, except ye be converted, and become as little children, ye shall not enter into the kingdom of heaven."

I went hiking with a group recently. There were twin boys (about six years old) in our group hiking with their parents. It was a 90-minute hike and their mom was completely petrified of heights, but her boys were fearless. There were no reservations that plagued their confidence. Several times the mother called out, "Slow down boys, please stop boys, don't go so fast boys, you can't do that boys!" I was so inspired by their strength.

Just as children move with such trust and confidence, like I did and the twin boys did in those experiences, I am reminded that God wants us to be like that as adults; totally leaning on Him and not on our own understanding. Sometimes God asks things of me that appear unattainable, but when I trust Him, I see His faithfulness.

I have learned that no matter what this world hands me, there is destiny with my name on it. To get there, I just have to walk with no fear, worry, doubt or hesitation. God says to me, "I trust you, you can do this, I need you, I am here." No longer will I let my mistakes or the world yell to me, "Slow down, you can't do that, please stop, don't do that!"

Now, because of God, I am changed. I am exclusive, rare, effervescent, vivacious, insuppressible, uncontainable, and unrestrainable!

Questions:

1. At some point in life, have you given your confidence away?
2. How can you regain your confidence?
3. What fears do you need to let go of so you can totally trust God and allow yourself to regain confidence in Him?

Trisha Ferguson - Restoring God's Original

"God is Spirit, and those who worship Him must worship in spirit and truth."

John 4:24

Chapter 5

I've often wondered how much of me is what God originally created, versus how much is the result of the *world* coming after me, and then God re-creating that original.

"You were born gutsy," my mother has always told me. Apparently, I came out of the womb in full voice, ready to meet the world with energy and determination. I truly believe, in that moment, I was God's perfect original creation, created to make His praise glorious. My nature was set - I was determined, bold, confident, musically gifted, and driven. And then the *world* hit me like the cold slap on the rear!

My nature was about to collide with my nurture. In many ways, the nurture of my mom's constant love encouraged and built up many of God's perfect characteristics in me. But there were many things in my life that would also force me to overcome. In my family of origin, I have always felt like my personality and spirit didn't fit. I grew up with a very loving mother, a sweet dad and a sister who I looked up to for everything. But all three of those people were very different from me. My dad and sister were quite shy, and my mom, although extroverted, was not a risk-taker and highly values security. I, on the other hand, have always wanted to be on the edge; wanting to take the risk and obtain the reward. I want the excitement and adventures; to try new things, build things from the ground up and be my own free spirit, whatever that may bring. I value personal freedom, and even as a child wanted to create, artistically, and to dream. But I was never encouraged to dream. I was told what my limits were and how to adjust to the world, instead of forcing the world to adjust to the God in me.

At 17, my boyfriend's parents encouraged me to audition for a music scholarship to attend a nearby private university. Hesitant and scared (which has always been a constant in my life), I did it anyway, and ended up being offered almost a full-ride. At 19, still in school, I got a job working for a small corporation and fell in love with the work. At 21, as a single woman, I purchased my first house.

The same week I bought that house, I walked into Capital Christian Center, still where I attend and serve today.

That very week I started to exceed my nurture. No one in my family had ever gone beyond that in the American dream. I had some education, a secure job and a house. My nurture had told me that was the end. And then I started to hear messages at church like, "God has placed dreams in you," and, "Pull your faith up." In four short years, by age 25, I purchased the company I had been working for and became the sole owner. Between 25 and 35, I expanded the business by buying out another business, eliminated outside vendors by purchasing our own printing equipment, tripled sales revenue and staff, and invested in my second commercial building. My dreams kept getting bigger, and at each level and in each season, God was re-creating His original.

At the same time my career was expanding, I was discovering my true self. My God-ordained dreams were birthed by serving God's house with my musical gifts. Worship became everything to me. It is where I felt the most alive and the place I finally fit. God began to speak to me about the future, and those dreams have overtaken my spirit and are aligned perfectly with me, the re-created original.

Only one thing was missing. At 28, I was stuck. Having already been through a heart-breaking divorce that was riddled with substantial infidelity and betrayal, I was convinced marriage was also an area where I just didn't fit. What man wouldn't betray my trust? What man wanted a gutsy, aggressive, driven woman? What man wouldn't be threatened by the big dreams?

Aaron! God's perfection at its finest. God sent me Aaron, and as a woman, I needed him. Without him coming into my life, I would have missed the greatest part of the dream. As I sit here pregnant with our second child, I am overwhelmed by the confidence he has in himself: that confidence has given me a greater sense of myself and the dream of motherhood. Aaron is my protector, my leader, my shelter, and my partner in every true sense. He loves that I dream. He has never been threatened by my successes and never puts the God-dream in between us. His love is what I now know as Jesus' love in my life. I will forever be complete because of Aaron and Jesus.

As I move forward on the journey, I have decided that every single day and in every season *He* will continue to re-create the original unique and unstoppable woman I am destined to be! So many more dreams…

Questions:

1. In what way has your nature collided with your nurture?
2. Who could you surround yourself with that can help develop what's in you?
3. Will you allow the Holy Spirit to give you big dreams?

Christina Sipe - The Beach

"Oh, give thanks to the Lord, for He is good! For His mercy endures forever."

Psalm 136:1

Chapter 6

I like to travel twice a year to the same beach. I've been asked why I love that particular beach so much and return so frequently. Wouldn't I want to go somewhere else? No, I have shared this beach with my husband of 16 years, my children, my momma, my extended family, and my closest friends. I run during its sunrise and sit in its warm sand during spectacular sunsets. Everything about this beach – the smell, the sun, the sounds, the feel of sand and crashing waves – are extremely comforting for me. While all these aspects make me cherish this place, meeting God there is what really makes it feel like home. It's the place where I have gone to grieve, grow, heal, and rejoice.

A few years ago, following a very busy and stressful time, an unexpected change occurred in my life. It was the breakup of a business partnership. It wasn't fair, and it wasn't my choice. However, sometimes God asks us to give up the plan we have for our life because He has a greater plan, if only we'll surrender ours. As a family, we took the step of faith to surrender our plan, knowing sacrifice and pain would come, but also knowing God would bring us out on the other side. We returned to our special beach, and I grieved quietly.

Upon returning home, I was exhausted and spread thin. I was busy with my usual mom, wife, work and volunteer responsibilities, but the addition of business changes, disappointment and unsettled decisions allowed the enemy to creep in and establish a stronghold. Before I knew it, I was battling a full-blown anxiety disorder. I lost 25 pounds in less than six weeks (which I did not need to lose), woke up every morning counting the hours until I could go back to bed because I physically felt awful, got up only for my must-do activities so nobody would really see how bad it had gotten, and wrote down even the most basic tasks so I could function. I forced myself to attend two Bible studies a week, put on my "doing" face for everyone else, then went home again and climbed into bed until my kids got home. Only my husband and a close friend knew the true severity of my situation. Outward looks can be deceiving, and I was able to do just enough to maintain the outside which kept probing questions at bay.

I was paralyzed. Guilty thoughts and condemnation plagued me.

"I am a Christian, and I shouldn't feel like this."

"I should be stronger than this."

"If I just pray more, read more, do more for God, serve more, and just be good…"

Unfortunately, a biological change had also occurred in my body, and I wasn't getting better regardless of how much I prayed or read my Bible. The level of daily anxiety I was dealing with took physical toll on my body, and I was no longer functioning normally. Anxiety is a taboo topic to talk about, particularly in church circles. People quietly medicate, treating the symptoms, but don't address the root problem. I was ashamed.

Thankfully, my husband sought out help, and soon I was in counseling with a Spirit-filled Christian counselor. It was a safe place to discuss my issues and have someone help me address them. I did use medication to assist with my physical symptoms. Initially, I beat myself up for having to medicate. That meant I was weak, right? And, that I didn't have enough faith? That's another lie from the enemy that I had to overcome.

I went to the beach again, this time to grow. I prayed and cried out to God to take away these things I had been trying to remove by myself. I began researching and reading, not only my Bible, but other books about people that had fought similar struggles and were still used by God. It's amazing how many Christians, even in leadership positions, have been affected by this same issue. By being transparent, sharing our struggles and being "real" with one another sheds light on what the enemy wants to shame us with.

By His grace, I have overcome and am wiser, more compassionate and stronger. I've always been an independent, "pull yourself up by the bootstraps," get-it-done kind of girl, and yet I just couldn't do this one on my own. God has shown me grace and compassion during this journey, though I didn't deserve it. Now I can extend His grace and compassion to others, knowing their battle may not be the same as mine, but it's a battle nonetheless. Without a helping hand and an encouraging word, sometimes you can't "just get over it."

A verse that I repeated during this time was 2 Corinthians 12:9; however I love the entire passage as it reads in THE MESSAGE Bible:

I was given the gift of a handicap to keep me in constant touch with my limitations. Satan's angel did his best to get me down; what he in fact did was push me to my knees. No danger then of walking around high and mighty! At first I didn't think of it as a gift, and begged God to remove it. Three times I did that, and then he told me,
My grace is enough; it's all you need.
My strength comes into its own in your weakness.
Once I heard that, I was glad to let it happen. I quit focusing on the handicap and began appreciating the gift. It was a case of Christ's strength moving in on my weakness. Now I take limitations in stride, and with good cheer, these limitations that cut me down to size— abuse, accidents, opposition, bad breaks. I just let Christ take over! And so the weaker I get, the stronger I become.
2 Corinthians 12:7-10

We can't earn His all-sufficient grace. He gives it to us freely. So, the next time I went to the beach was to heal. As I watched each wave washing my footprints away, it was just like Him; sweeping in and carrying away the past, as far as the East is to the West, leaving no sign that it had ever been. I let go of the memories of sin, past hurts and regrets and began to build a new identity in Him. In my weakness, His strength was revealed.

This year, I returned to the beach to rejoice. I'm so grateful God has forever changed me, and hope that through sharing my experience, someone else will be encouraged. Everyone needs their own "beach" where they meet with God.

Questions:

1. Are you willing to reveal or expose the strongholds in your life?
2. What stronghold or sin are you hiding or masking from others?
3. Will you take the step today to reach out or allow someone to reach in and help you?

Krista Dunk - Letting Go of Timidity & Letting God be Big

"A little one shall become a thousand, and a small one a strong nation. I, the Lord, will hasten it in its time."

Isaiah 60:22

Chapter 7

I always knew God made me unique. Even as a child, this truth was written on my heart. However, for much of my life, I was definitely stoppable.

I lived small. I felt small. Unique and small…that was me. Even though I was packed with personal potential and giftedness, I never came close to reaching it, I lacked the desire to discover it and had no understanding about how to find or express it.

As a young person, although I was well-liked and was a good student, I was incredibly timid. My goals looked something like this: avoid confrontation, be sure everyone likes me, work to be perfect in every endeavor, work to keep things secure and unchanging, and most of all, avoid anything that required using my voice. I had a box, and I was satisfied staying in it. My comfort zone "box" worked for me, most of the time.

The enemy was happy to keep me quiet and living small. I was repressed…oppressed. Only now do I see that the enemy was attacking an area where my future calling would be – expression and my voice. I was angry inside and unable to express my feelings. I literally did not know how to. At times, I could not make the words I wanted to say escape my mouth. It was like I had a lid firmly covering over and closing off my ability to express myself. Strangely, as all this was happening inside, from the outside, my life was fairly normal, safe, I was a good kid, and most things appeared to be fine.

Due to my parents divorcing when I was 12 and leaving the church I grew up in, all of my teen years were spent away from church. I made some good choices, like keeping my grades up and staying involved in extracurricular activities, and I made some poor choices, such as destructive relationships with boys and compromising my values to fit in. Thankfully, God was in control. At age 21, newly married, I started attending church again and rededicated my life to Christ shortly thereafter.

Every-so-often, people would challenge my comfort zone. My husband wouldn't let me hide my feelings and opinions from him. His patience drew me out of my shell, bit-by-bit. When I was 25, my mother and sister talked me into singing a trio with them at church…on a microphone…in front of people…God forbid! Well, I did it, but it stressed me out so badly that my knees knocked, voice cracked and stomach churned. Another time, a worship pastor commented that I needed to be on stage with the team during services. I responded under my breath, "Only if I can put a bag on my head…" Staying small and inconspicuous was my safe and undemanding role, or so I thought.

By speaking to me and showing me His plan for my life, one piece at a time, God started changing my self-image to match His perspective. Even when I would respond, "Who, me?" because of small thinking, He made it clear, "No, not you by yourself, but in *My* mighty power and through *My* Spirit." Yes, without Him, I truly am small. With Him, all things are possible!

He was calling me to sing on the worship team, be a public speaker, write a book, be a leader, and other petrifying things! Even as my world and opportunities began to brim with promise, deep down my self-confidence still wavered. Waves of anxiety frequently plagued me, causing physical symptoms. Could I really handle these big dreams and assignments He was giving me? Was I qualified for this amount of vision?

During a virtual ministry conference I hosted, one of the speakers talked us through a visualization exercise that went something like this: "Imagine yourself on a beautiful beach. Hear the waves crashing. Feel the ocean breeze and the warm sand between your toes. You turn and look down the beach and see Jesus afar off. He is walking towards you. Your heart leaps and you run to Him. As you reach Him, He opens His arms to embrace you. While in His embrace, He says, 'Daughter, what worries do you have in your heart?'"

As I listened and imagined this scene for myself, I was surprised at my instant answer: "I'm afraid to be big." He lovingly answered, "Just let *Me* be big."

God has helped me become aware of my tendency to become anxious. Anxiety is *not* a way of life. Anyone who struggles with it knows it can sneak up at any time. Sometimes it accompanies the need to be in control, but now I know to turn over *all* my cares, worries and stress to God. I discover where the anxiety is stemming from and declare my trust in God for that area of my life. He is always faithful to give my heart peace.

As I look back on my journey, my life is remarkably different today. Right now, I have a firm understanding of His calling for me, and I'm stepping out into new places along that calling's path. It feels like standing high atop an overlook, with an expansive territory in full view. I'm on fire with excitement about what He has for my future and for those He's called me to impact.

Complacency, small living/thinking and mediocrity are not okay anymore. I lived like that for much too long. I can't continue to live forward, while engaging old habits and mindsets. My sense of "normal" living, my capacity and what's possible continues to shift!

To me, being unique means having the deep understanding that God has designed me for a special place within His purposes and there's no one else quite like me. Each of us has a contribution to the world that cannot be duplicated.

Being unstoppable starts with a decision first, then building an enduring strength which comes from understanding what makes you unique and knowing that God is with you. A woman who is unique and unstoppable can't help but minister and impact others with her gifts, and she expresses herself with wisdom. This has become my goal and focus.

Although I've come a long way, my journey is not complete. I haven't "arrived." Until the day my spirit separates from this temporary home and I see the Lord face to face, I will be on this unique and unstoppable journey. It's surprising and wonderful what God can do with a life dedicated to Him.

Questions:

1. In what areas of your life have you lived quiet and small?
2. Could these *timid* areas you've identified be the very places that God is calling you to?
3. After you did the visualization exercise of Jesus on the beach, what was your answer?

Danielle Payment - When Leaders Lose Their Way

"Not by might nor by power, but by My Spirit, says the Lord of hosts."

Zechariah 4:6

Chapter 8

I was seven months pregnant with my fourth child when my husband and I knew it was time for me to transition to being at home. For the previous fourteen years, I served my church as a full time youth pastor and then became the women's pastor. Staying home was one of the most difficult transitions I've ever made. During this huge season of change, my self-discovery began...

Once I was home, my identity began to unravel. Unaware of it at that time, my entire identity had been wrapped up in my role as pastor and leader. It was all that I knew and all that I loved. "Pastor Danielle" had risen in importance above my husband, above my family, and yes, above my God. What I *did* was who I had become. I will never forget the day the Lord revealed to me how my busyness had hurt my husband. For the first time, I literally felt my husband's pain.

I had lost someone a year earlier; someone who was very important to me. I had not even begun to process or deal with it, until I transitioned, and there was nothing for me "to do" than to be home and take care of my family...and *think*. Each day, during the kids' naptime, I spent quiet time with God. Some days were spent just lying on the floor and crying until my insides hurt. I had completely shut my heart from me hearing the Lord or seeking the Lord, I had become *one of those leaders* that I always heard about and was warned about; the kind of leader that only sought the Lord for messages, events and crisis. Sadly, I adopted that behavior, and with adopting that behavior I gave my confidence away. My outward behavior was fueled by inside inadequacies and insecurities. I was snared. Every time I produced something, met a goal or accomplished something, it was for the challenge and the approval of man verses the motive of loving God and His Kingdom. So, my idol became what I did more than who I loved and why I did it. I had lost my way. The praise of accomplishing and the opportunities that opened due to performing well fed me more than my relationships with God or my husband did. I didn't even consider either of them, not knowing that I was completely out of order. It's funny...God will have His way. He knew that I dearly loved Him, but I had just lost *my* way!

During this season, as my heart began to open back up to the Lord, He lovingly began to reveal my own wrong-doing. I began to take responsibility for where I found myself. I will never forget that day of repentance between me and God. I'm pretty sure I did not get off of the floor until everything within me said I was sorry for all of it. Sorry for my behavior, sorry for placing everything above Him.

I committed to never again live this way. From that day on, God would always be first, and I am learning how to love and serve my husband, and also care about what he values. I thank God that He revealed all of this, and that I was able to turn from my ways and begin the hard work of changing. This brought so much healing to my soul, my marriage, my family, and most importantly, my personal relationship with the Lord. I placed my identity in Him and Him alone; not in what I do or don't do.

These were precious days spent in the presence of God. I even started going for a run and listening to uplifting music on my iPod in the afternoons when my husband came home from work. Mary J. Blige's "Breakthrough" and India Arie's "Beautiful Flower" albums were especially powerful for me. I would have "church" during my daily run. God began to help me dream again!

On one of my runs, my eldest son came with me on his bike. As I ran, he'd get about 100 yards ahead of me and I would yell, "Levi! Wait up – don't get out of reach of my voice." I trained him to ride 100 yards, then stop and check in to make sure I was still with him. All of a sudden, I heard the Holy Spirit say, *"This is exactly what I am doing with you daughter. You are going to learn how to stay in step with Me, and when you forget and get ahead of Me, stop and check in."* From that moment on, I have spent every day learning how to stay in step with the Holy Spirit – not ahead of Him or behind Him, but in-step. And when I charge ahead or start to lose my way, I now know to stop and check in immediately. Even now as I write this, I realize how far I've come because of checking in as I start each day and throughout the whole day!

At the end of two years, I returned to ministry, but this time with my identity firmly planted in God, and I am strong in Him. God has a funny way of being jealous about that which He has created. I could not have known the kind of powerful life He had in store for me, my family and my church.

God has restored my life. I am celebrating twenty years of marriage to the husband of my youth, we have our own company, and we are blessed to serve our local church together with our four children. And I have the most beautiful friends that anyone could ever ask for. When I gave my all to God, He gave it all back to me.

Questions:

1. What is your identity found in; in the things you do or in God who created you?
2. Do you have a time set aside *daily* to be with the Lord in a personal way?
3. Can you let go and give it *all* to Him, so He can give it *all* back to you?

Tammy Redmon - Abused, Abandoned, Adored!

"And the very hairs on your head are all numbered. So don't be afraid; you are more valuable to God than a whole flock of sparrows."

Luke 12:7

Chapter 9

If you're anything like me, you fell in love with a 7-inch, felt Jesus stuck to a Sunday school storyboard. It was in an old country grange church that I felt truly loved for the first time. I was just five years old, and I can still see the teacher, smell the room and hear the piano pounding out *Jesus Loves Me* as if it were yesterday.

My love (or maybe it was a crush) for Jesus grew through my younger years, and today, in my mid 40's, I can honestly say I don't recall a time when I haven't loved the Lord. Even in the depths of despair, pain and sorrow, I held onto this song:

Jesus loves me this I know,
For the Bible tells me so.
Little ones to Him belong,
They are weak but He is strong.

I survived because of those words. No matter what, I knew my "felt" Jesus loved me. But now God has shown me I am more than loved: I am *adored*!

Being raised by a single mother in the 70's was a very interesting experience. At that time, women were exploring their freedom and creating new identities for themselves. The "free love," burn-your-bra time period exposed children to things that were, quite simply, not of God. At least that's how it was at my house. Alcohol flowed freely, and partying went on all night. As a child, I witnessed and experienced abuse at many levels; abuse of body, abuse of women, abuse of alcohol, and abuse of whatever made them feel good or covered up emotional pain. Accepting abuse is what I learned. Abuse was my "normal."

I left home the day after I graduated high school, and that day could not have come soon enough. I wanted (and needed) to escape the abuse I'd been enduring my entire life. It was my time to go out into the world and make things happen for me. My heart was filled with immense dreams, and I knew nothing would stand in the way of attaining them! So off I went to far away parts of the country: Alaska's Bering Sea.

Shortly after arriving on a little island called Alyeska, I discovered...boys. Much of my teen years I'd avoided boys. To me they weren't safe. So many boys and men abused me in my early years that I wanted nothing to do with any of them, until I met one young man who made me feel very special. He delighted me with gifts and attention. He sent me flowers from the mainland. He sent gifts to my office, and one evening showed up in a snow storm to bring me hot chocolate. At 18, I was rather smitten with the attention.

Then, "normal" came to visit. One day while driving we had a rather *loud* discussion, and in his anger, he threw an object from the window. I remember saying to myself, "All men must throw things when they get angry." It was normal to me. When he asked me to marry him after dating only four months, I immediately said yes and couldn't wait to call my mom. I found someone she would really like. Why? Because he was just like all the men I saw her with as I grew up - abusers. I welcomed it.

During that time, I'd found a little church to attend and heard messages about being a good wife that submitted to her husband. I followed the path that seemed right to follow, and we were married.

As with most abusive relationships, the intensity increased after we said "I do," and the velocity grew even greater when I was pregnant with our first child. I felt so stuck. I picked this man. We were married and no matter what, I could not leave. God did not approve of divorce, right? Divorce was a sin in my eyes, and everything I found to read confirmed it. To me, I thought being abused was a way of life for everyone. I had no other frame of reference to draw from. There was the public face and the private face that I put on inside the four walls of our bedroom.

Over time, the beatings and the tearing apart of my self-esteem had a numbing affect. I had my outside face and my inside voice. For years I went through the motions, looking for the changes in my husband's eyes or a sweaty forehead to predict what my night would be like. It was my routine. I had abandoned all aspects of self. Even though I was a member of a lovely church near Seattle and attended women's luncheons and Bible studies, knowing my Heavenly

Father's love for me had been lost. I let go of trying to feel His embrace and His strength in my life. I felt like a failure. And even though *Jesus loves me* and *He is strong when I am weak,* I didn't see myself as loveable. Every day the man on earth (that I thought was from God) told me that I wasn't, so it must have been true, right? Wrong!

Through the faces of my young children, God showed me how much he adored us. He wanted them to be safe and for me to break the cycle of abuse that consumed my whole life. A single moment changed me forever. *"Mommy, if you wouldn't make Daddy so angry, he wouldn't have to hit you."*

My God…what had I done? The Lord had given me two beautiful little cherubs in my children, whom I adored. I was alive for them. I would never abuse or abandon them. How is it that I'd placed them into the very same "abuse is normal" environment that I grew up in? At that catalyst moment, Jesus came in like a roaring lion and fought to get us out.

Jesus went to battle for me. He was my strength to pack up and leave. He was stronger than me when I needed a fresh new touch of heaven. He put people all around me to tell me I was worthy of a life where I was adored and safe. Jesus painted a new picture for me of what life could be by setting me free from the chains that bound me to my past.

When I took hold of the new story that Jesus was telling me, when I got a new picture of life with Jesus as my rock, I never looked back. And if I began to turn my head, I heard the words of my little boy ringing in my ear or saw the image of my daughter being slapped in the face by a man. The love of my Heavenly Father *was* raining down and protecting me. His love was so deep for me. Who am I *not* to love Him just as much!

Even when I fail today, I know Jesus loves me, and when I'm weak He floods in to be my strength. "He knew me before I was formed and knows the number of hairs on my head." The pain of the years lost has diminished over time. They are years restored to me as I see the loving, healthy lives my children have today. Breaking the generational curse was the call on my life, and I am blessed that my battle was victorious because of Jesus – my Rock, Redeemer, Shield and Lover of my soul.

Questions:

1. Do you see yourself as loveable?
2. In what way can you relate to having your *outside face* on, yet with an *inside voice* that portrays something different?
3. What situations or environments seem "normal" to you, but you're discovering they are actually harmful?

Sherry Elliott - Not Even a Hint of Smoke

"For we are God's workmanship, created in Christ Jesus for good works, which God prepared beforehand that we should walk in them."

Ephesians 2:10

Chapter 10

One of my favorite Bible stories growing up was the story of Shadrach, Meshach and Abednego. Perhaps it was the challenge of saying their names as a child, which inevitably got a laugh when I'd mistakenly say, "in bed we go!" Maybe it was the images in my mind of these brave young men facing the fiery furnace and the look on King Nebuchadnezzar's face when he saw that the flames did not burn them. Ultimately, it is a story of overcoming the odds and standing strong in your faith. But, it wasn't until I grew older that their story took on a deeper meaning for me. I, too, have faced my fiery furnace, but I stand here today with not even the hint of smoke.

I would love to be able to say my family environment was nurturing, safe and secure, but we do not get to choose our families. They say abuse is a vicious cycle, and I know this to be true. My mother was seventeen when she married my father to escape the abuse she endured at home. She thought he was her knight in shining armor, but what she didn't see was his armor was also tarnished by verbal and physical abuse from his mother. So there you have it; two wounded people running into each other's arms to escape their abusive families and start one of their own.

What I did not know at the time was that God sees the end from beginning. Just as He was with Shadrach, Meshach and Abednego during their trials, He was with me too. He knew everything I'd ever go through, every harsh word spoken over me and saw every hand that afflicted me. Even so, He knew in the end I would overcome.

One early recollection was at age three. I vividly remember my sisters and I being locked in our room; locked from the outside so we could not leave. We had come to know that this meant Dad was going to beat our mother. We heard screaming, yelling and crying through our bedroom door, and the three of us were huddled together, bound in fear and shame. I remember on another occasion, he forgot to lock our door. My sisters and I decided we'd try to stop him from hurting mom. We grabbed every stuffed animal we could find, stormed out of our room, and threw whatever we could at our father while yelling, "Get off of mommy!" Our efforts only delayed the inevitable. We were smacked across our faces, scooped up and thrown back into our room. The fighter within me was born that day.

My mother finally got up enough courage to leave my father, and she moved us from one coast to the other when I was ten. At last we were free from the physical abuse, but my mother's own scars ran deep. When times of stress overwhelmed my mom, her weapon of choice was verbal assaults. Those emotional scars took much longer to heal.

Looking back, I believe my mom was doing her best to make a better life for us. I am grateful my mom insisted we go to church on Sundays. My father had never permitted it. Sundays became my refuge and place of joy, learning, playing, singing, and peace. At thirteen, and armed with new understanding, I chose to become part of God's family and was baptized. I still remember peace washing over me the day I prayed a simple prayer accepting Jesus as my Savior.

I wish I could tell you I obeyed God and followed Him wholeheartedly afterward. I tried to understand God as my Heavenly Father, but my image of a father was distorted. I also struggled with my own identity. Just as Shadrach, Meshach and Abednego were renamed and stripped of their God identity (Daniel 1:1-7), my identity in God had been stripped away as a child. In my sophomore year of high school, I hung around the wrong crowd and got caught up in drinking and drugs. I was starving to be part of any family other than my own.

At sixteen, I moved in with a family from our church who knew our family dynamics. This was the first time I experienced a healthy family. I stopped hanging out with my party friends, began focusing on my future, and returned to church. At seventeen, I joined the Air Force knowing it would be my chance at a new life. If I wanted to have a different outcome for my future, I had to be the one to break the cycle of abuse. God placed that desire in me. As soon as I got a permanent duty station, I sought counseling. This was such a healing time for me. After a year of self-discovery and healing, I was finally able to forgive myself and forgive those who wronged me. I also began reconciling the broken relationship with my mother. It was during this time I met my future husband, Brian.

Brian was God's gift to me. I'd never met anyone like him. I typically dated boys who treated me badly. I allowed it because part of me felt needed in their brokenness. Brian was emotionally solid, and that frightened me. I played hard to get, tried scaring him off with my games, but he saw through my tough exterior and I knew he was the one. We got married when I turned twenty three.

Looking back, I realize I had come out of the fiery furnace, but was still bound in fear and shame. This affected our first three years of marriage. I had a temper, and my harsh words brought out the worst in Brian. As much as I verbally assaulted him during our fights, he never raised a hand to me. He was not that kind of man, but he sure broke some furniture back then! He'd retreat to the garage, and I'd hear him smashing things. We can laugh about it now, but it wasn't funny back then.

We both agreed to marriage counseling which showed us the root of our stress and fighting. Communication was our issue to tackle, but I knew something was still missing: church. I longed for the peace of God in my life. I made the decision to go back to church, but Brian didn't have that same desire. He was raised Catholic, and while he had a good foundation of faith, attending church wasn't important to him. I did everything to beg, persuade and manipulate him to go with me. One day, I heard a voice in my head say, "Stop asking, and just go on your own." So I did just that, week after week. One Sunday, for no particular reason, Brian got up and said, "I think I'll go with you today." I did my best not to do cartwheels and flips, but inside I was rejoicing! I knew God promised that if I delighted in Him, He would grant me my heart's desire for a God-serving, loving family. Church became a weekly routine, and as we grew our faith, our relationship grew closer too. We decided to follow God from that day forward. I was 27.

Over the last 21 years together, all of our miraculous stories point back to one decision; giving God our all, surrendering everything, and holding nothing back. When I look at my children, I reflect on the life God has given me. The fear and shame that once bound me is gone. I am free! God saved me, and who the Son sets free is free indeed!

Now it's my turn to let my light shine for those who need hope. Like Shadrach, Meshach and Abednego who were bound, perhaps you are bound too. With Jesus, it's possible to go through the fire and come out unscathed. My identity has become beautifully entwined with God's. I have found my purpose, and the vicious cycle of abuse is defeated. I now serve as the children's pastor at my church, and have the honor of sharing God's love in amazing ways to many children. Life has been a magnificent journey with God. I survived the fiery furnace with not even a hint of smoke, and so can you.

Questions:

1. Do you have painful memories of abuse?
2. Could your image of Father God be distorted due to abuse from, or shortcomings of, influential people in your past?
3. Will you give God your all, surrender everything and hold nothing back?

Melissa Wade - From Brokenness, to Healed & Unstoppable

"Those who are planted in the house of the Lord shall flourish in the courts of our God."

Psalm 92:13

Chapter 11

Who would have known that God could take an insecure, timid girl and turn her into a confident woman of ministry and vision? Only by the loving grace of God could this be possible.

I used to live a life of insecurity. I didn't know who I was, and tried to find my completeness through the approval of others; primarily from my father and my husbands.

Dad was a good, respectable man, who provided for my needs the best he knew how. This was a challenge for him because he never had a good role model for a father. When my parents divorced and moved far apart, I only saw my Dad when he could fly into town. Although he met my physical needs and provided for me financially, he didn't know how to meet my other needs; needs a girl can only receive from a loving father who speaks words of approval and encouragement.

Because approval and encouragement were lacking in my life, I looked for those needs to be met through my boyfriends and husbands. Out of a need to feel important and wanted, I found boyfriends and husbands who "needed" me. My mission was to be there for them and help them, or should I say, "fix" them. Each boyfriend and husband had a desperate need for someone to be there for them. Being needed made me feel important. Little did I know that it wasn't me they needed, it was God.

Even though I had known the Lord since I was 19, many of those years were spent losing myself in bad relationships. I always tried to be what a guy wanted me to be and I always failed. Nothing I did was ever good enough. Eventually, I stopped trying, because each attempt ended with criticism. If only I had known that I was a daughter of the King. But I was clueless. It wasn't until God showed me who I really was that I finally healed from the effects of these unhealthy relationships.

I wondered why I suffered in bad relationships. I did not do what the Bible said even though I thought I was. I did much of the obvious stuff, "thou shalt not steal," "thou shalt not murder," etc. However, I wasn't understanding or practicing the not-so-obvious stuff, such as "those who are planted in the house of God will flourish," and "those who lose their life for my sake will find it." Without realizing it, I made my boyfriends and husbands idols in my life. I put them before God and even tried playing God in *their* lives. Had I put God first, I would have discovered my identity and perhaps avoided some of this pain.

Three months of depression followed a very painful second divorce, and I finally took a step of faith and got involved in a local church. First, I started serving on the worship team, where God did some amazing healing through worshipping Him. His Word is true when it says, "The joy of the Lord is my strength." It was a great time of healing. Then I served on the greeting team, hosted a small group in my home and eventually served on the prayer team. Serving and ministering to others is when the healing of my own hurts, habits and hang-ups took place. I lost my life for His sake during this period of time, and God poured into me. My biggest leaps of spiritual growth have happened while serving and ministering to others.

While serving was important, I sometimes tried to serve and minister out of my own strength, and would get frustrated and exhausted. Spending time with Him, *alone*, has been crucial to my spiritual growth, maturity and ability to do His work. It is when I make time to get alone with God that He speaks to me, gives me direction, and lets me know about changes I need to make. Going to church is good and so is serving, but to truly know God on an intimate level and to fulfill the plans He has for us, we must spend quality time with Him by reading His Word and worshipping Him. This is what it means to seek Him diligently. Those who seek Him with their whole heart *will* find Him. And when I am alone with Him, I have learned to wait expectantly with paper and pen in hand to write down what He speaks.

I'm excited about the future God has for me. He's stirring me in the areas of helping to plant new churches and missions work. God has used the last several years, and different ministries that I've been involved with, to prepare me, and now He is putting it on my heart to move forward. Had I not spent time alone with Him and sought Him with my whole heart, I would not have heard this important calling. Although I'm not exactly sure where I'll end up, He's told me not to delay and to get a passport. "Yes, Lord, here I am…send me!" May this also be the cry of *your* heart. And when it is, watch and see what amazing things He will do through you and for you.

Questions:

1. Do you wish you had more encouragement in your life?
2. What kind of insecurities do you have that produce the need for approval?
3. How can you get the right kind of encouragement that is needed in your life?

Carla Baptiste - Dancing in Freedom

*"Then David danced before the Lord
with all his might."*

2 Samuel 6:14

Chapter 12

I like to dance. There's something that happens to my spirit when I hear funky music. It gets me going! Lately, I don't even care whether it's at the mall, waiting in line at the grocery store, getting gas or who's watching. Music moves me. I automatically move to any music that I hear or to the song playing in my heart. When I read the Bible story about David dancing for the Lord so passionately that he danced out of his clothes, it always puts a smile on my face. Instantly, I think I'm one of his distant relatives who received that dancing gene! Praise Him, somebody!

Thinking back, dancing and singing used to be very difficult for me. One day, my cousins came to visit, and my family wanted us to dance. I couldn't do it. I felt awkward, timid and out of place for some reason. I broke down and cried. Because I am so much taller than normal, people teased me a lot. They'd also put me down about my very dark skin color. Even now I can hear the taunts, which solidified my insecurities, "You are so dark we can only see your eyes and teeth at night!" or "Your feet are so big, we can see them coming before we see you!" Adding to the self-image problems, in my own eyes, I had the biggest nose of any person alive. As I grew older though, I realized my father and I have the same nose, and it's really not so bad. But, back then, I cried frequently about feeling "different" and standing out in uncomfortable ways.

Our Sunday school teacher heard something in me when I sang. He asked me do a solo. I told him no – I would certainly not sing by myself. However, I would do it only if I could sing a duet with the other girl, also named Carla, at church. Things changed when I entered high school and there were school dances and choirs to join. I was the loudest singer but refused to ever do a solo. Also, I discovered that I could dance, and dance really well. One time, I even won a contest for being the best dancer.

My dad was a professional singer and a well-known DJ who worked in one of the hottest clubs in Bermuda. My friends and I were in that club every Thursday, without fail. Once we were inside, I never sat down. He sang at events all over the region, and he was fun to watch. He made me proud.

Recently, dad sent me three CD's of "old school" music…you know, from back in the day when they sang *for real*, with *real* instruments, and you could understand what they were saying! One night, as we played the CD's, a song came on by Rick James. My husband, Mac, was ironing clothes, and I decided to dance in the door way. Every time the music went into the chorus, I'd slide to one side of the door frame and kick my leg up, and then move back quickly and continue dancing. Mac just looked at me and started to laugh, telling me, "Don't hurt yourself!" Sometimes I'll put the music on, move the coffee table out of the way and dance until I get tired, or until they play a song that's too slow. For me, dancing is a release, it puts a smile on my face and it definitely takes me out of my comfort zone, if I let it.

Years ago, we went to an outdoor music festival here in Washington State where an awesome Christian group was playing. We were sitting on top of a hill, taking the music in, and I looked over and saw a five year old little girl who looked like she wanted to dance. I motioned to her to start dancing, and she just smiled. So, I got up and held my hand out. Well, it was *on*! That little girl and I danced together for the longest time. Dancing has a way of bringing people together, no matter the age or race, experienced or not. It's just fun.

How many times in my past did I sit out and miss out? Dancing takes me to another place; a place of joy. I used to think, "I'm not good enough," "I can't do it" (whatever the challenge might have been) or "People will look at me and laugh." Honestly, maybe they do, but so what. Maybe they have insecurities! I've realized we all have something we wish we could do just like someone else, but we must also realize that we weren't meant to do the same things that someone else is doing.

God made us in His image, and we are to do what He created us to do. I'm not hiding anymore. I'm tired of sitting on the sidelines wondering what could have been. I'm unique and called to do the will of God.

This past year, I was laid off from work. It turned out to be a blessing in disguise because I would have missed out on some wonderful nuggets from God. When I praise God, I do it with *all* that's within me, because I think about where I used to be. Since He breathes life in me each day, I want to praise Him with every fiber of my being. For me, that means to dance or sing, and read the Word of God. I don't know how to praise any other way.

Sitting on the sidelines is *not* an option for me anymore. If asked to do something, I'll do it. If I fail, that's okay; I'll retake the test and try again. If I fall, I'll get back up, stand up, fix myself and try again. Learning from our failures takes those pesky insecurities, fears and anything else negative and puts them on the sidelines where they belong.

At any gathering, just look for me. I'll be the one getting my groove and praise on for Jesus. Yes, sir, you can believe that! This is my time, our time, to do something we thought impossible and turn it into possible with God.

Questions:

1. Do you find freedom of expression when you're able to do the things you love?
2. Are you afraid to be free?
3. What is holding you back from living a free life?

Darci Coyne - I am Chosen

"For I know the plans I have for you, declares the Lord, plans to prosper you and not to harm you, plans to give you hope and a future."

Jeremiah 29:11

Chapter 13

Before my story begins, I can tell you how it ends: It ends with victory. Victory has not always been my story, however.

Many people view the Old Testament as a collection of old, boring stories. I, on the other hand, have always loved the Old Testament. It is full of people who have failed, just like me…people who have fears and concerns about life, just like me…people who have seen themselves as mediocre, just like me. It tells stories of people who *felt* very average, but accomplished great and mighty things through God. I take great comfort in one such story – the story of King David. King David's story is my story; a story of brokenness and sorrow, a story of redemption and triumph.

Like David, I grew up worshipping the Lord. I, too, was someone who loved the Lord with all my heart, yet made a devastating choice. And as sin always does, it crept further and further into the fabric of my being, permeating my soul until that final choice was made. In a pit of fear and despair, King David ultimately committed murder. Some may stop and be startled, wondering why I liken myself to David. The truth is, that while I may not have murdered a *person*, I am, nonetheless, a murderer. You see, I murdered a marriage. I am, like King David, an adulterer…a marriage is dead and gone because of me.

But, as we read further in David's story, we find that God used him as the greatest king in the Old Testament. He was, despite his failure, totally unstoppable. Often however, the journey to victory is paved with detours, bumps in the road and outright wrong-turns. My life is no exception.

Although I grew up loved by my family, I was a lonely child, always looking at life from the outside in. I didn't have a single friend until I was ten years old. I ate lunch alone. I played alone; always alone. They called me fat. They called me stupid. You know the kid that gets picked last for the sports team? That was me, *every single time*, and the sting of it never waned.

As a child, that kind of treatment shapes you because it seems to define your worth. I was perennially the *"un-chosen"* one, and that childhood pain seeped into the crevices of my heart, shaping the woman I would become. For years to follow, I labored under the shadow of being the *"un-chosen,"* and it seemed to me that *"un-chosen"* meant worthless.

Worthless and lonely is not a good combination. When you're seventeen years old and your prom date stands you up on what seems to be the most important night of your life, you begin to believe you really are fat, you really are stupid, and you really are *marred*. It became my truth. That was me...definitely not unique, and most certainly not unstoppable. The familiar sting eventually turned into a profound ache, and the pain seared deep into my heart, scarring the core of my soul.

As my teenage years gave way to adulthood, life became fuller and richer. I became a woman; a woman dedicated to doing things God's way, out of love for Him. And then one sweet day I met a "special someone." He, too, loved the Lord. As he prepared for a career in ministry, we quietly pondered whether we were meant to live our lives together, jointly serving God's plans and purposes. But then another day came; not another *sweet* day, rather a very bitter one. I got the word: *DEAD*. At twenty-eight years old, Michael was dead from a freak accident.

Grief and sorrow overwhelmed me. Depression gripped my heart. Hopelessness and despair hovered all around me, and a pain far greater than I'd ever known draped over me like a sickening blanket of grave clothes.

Once again that lonely little girl, now a woman, was alone, seemingly abandoned by the God she loved. Had *God* actually forgotten me and left me alone, just as the others had?

I feared I'd only know loneliness and the gut-wrenching pain of being *"un-chosen,"* forever. With the scars on my soul fully formed, I gave up. Pain and despair gave way to sin. I would do it *my* way now, not *His*. My course was set and in the years that followed I gave fully into sin in order to numb my pain, just as so many women do. I was twenty-nine years old and I exchanged my precious, hard-kept virginity for the arms of a man who would hold me tight, who would whisper words of love into my ear, and who would try and fill the excruciating hole in my heart.

As the years progressed, one man turned into two, two turned into three, and soon I met the one I wanted: *he* was the one I would choose. He stole my heart and appeared to be everything I had ever wanted, but a shroud of deceptive secrecy enveloped our love. By the time he told me he was married, the damage was done. My destructive choices had led me down a path...a path of adultery, and in the process I had shattered another woman's marriage. I, like King David, a lover of God, had murdered a marriage.

The problem with sin is that its soothing relief lasts only for a season, and then it gives way to death; spiritual, emotional, and mental death. The very choices we make to medicate our pain, ultimately end up enslaving us in shackles. Though the shackles are invisible to others, the bondage is painfully obvious to those of us wearing them. But remember, this story ends in victory.

If you could see the Bible I've had for years, you'd see many well-worn, tear-soaked, tape-repaired pages. The years of loneliness, heartache and failure thrust me to my knees in prayer, causing me to cry out to God and search His Word for direction and comfort. Those painful years beautified the pages of my Bible with a patina known only to broken people; known to those uniquely fashioned to be unstoppable through *Him* and His redemptive power of forgiveness.

Thankfully, God is not only forgiving, but He's magnificently restorative as well. As I became willing to humble myself before a loving God, He gently led me through a journey that healed my heart, and I personally experienced the beauty of Hosea 2:14-16. Jesus became the One who whispered tenderly to my heart, calling *Himself* my Husband, declaring that my "valley of trouble would become a door of hope." I waited 40 years, but then, in a moment of time, in walked a man named Dan Michael Coyne...the greatest man I've ever known. He *chose* me. Other than the Lord, he is the love of my life and I simply could not have imagined a man more wonderful for me than my precious Dan. I tell him often, "God saved the best for last." God chose a man for me who is equally unique, and together we walk, unstoppable, with a victorious Lord.

Questions:

1. What kind of failures are you currently dealing with in your life?
2. Do you see them as an opportunity?
3. Despite your failures, are you unstoppable like King David?

Deborah McLain - The Kaleidoscope Effect

"For the eyes of the Lord run to and fro throughout the whole earth, to show Himself strong on behalf of those whose heart is loyal to Him."

2 Chronicles 16:9

Chapter 14

I was eight years old when I heard the story of Jesus for the first time. We had just moved to a new town and my mother responded to an invitation to visit a local church. My family of six arrived and took up a whole pew in the balcony. The speaker stood next to a life-size wooden cross. He had a hammer in one hand and a huge stake in the other. As he told a vivid account of Jesus' suffering on the cross for my sins, the hammer echoed loudly through the room as he struck the nail, driving it into the wood. I was so moved. I believed him, and gave my heart to Jesus that day.

My life has taken some amazing twists and turns since then – some by choice, some not. But I can look back on all those years and see that God's hand was always on my life.

Moving every couple of years always made me the new kid in school. I remember the awkwardness and loneliness of that. I would talk to God a lot. During my junior high years, our family took our new-found faith to Liverpool, England, where my father was born and raised. For two years we were part of an outreach to inner city kids, and while there, reached out to my dad's ten brothers and sisters. I was perhaps too young to endure some of the hardships we experienced there though. My brothers and I worked hard to avoid the gangs at school, warding off their constant threats. There were times we did not succeed. We lived in a brick-rowed house in a poor neighborhood, with only coal heat and one cold water tap, and had to walk in the bitter cold and rain to a public bathhouse a couple times a week to take a bath. My parents had little money, but big faith, so my impressionable heart also witnessed many beautiful miracles and lives transformed by the love of Jesus.

In my early twenties, I returned to Liverpool for a visit, and while there met the "Pied Piper" of Liverpool, a passionate New Yorker working in the inner city, with whom I got swept up and married the following year. Two Americans in a foreign country, what can I say? Though we had a beautiful daughter together, the seven-year marriage was tumultuous. After two miscarriages, the sudden death of my youngest brother and my mother's attempted suicide all in one year, we finally separated. My faith was in the balance and would continue to be tested in new ways.

During the next 18 years of singleness and raising my daughter alone, the struggle was real. But, God faithfully put people in my path who strengthened me along the way. We moved from Washington State to New York so my daughter could be near her father. I enjoyed New York, but found myself again moving from place to place, working different jobs while trying to finish my degree, and running out of money and options time and time again. During one move, our car was packed up, ready to go, and my cell phone rang, "You can't come here, I am sorry, but you just can't come here now, it's not going to work out." I had nowhere to go and no idea what to do. I walked into a friend's backyard, crawled up into a lawn chair, pulled a blanket over my head and fell into deep despair.

Hours later, I was handed a small package that had come in the mail. It was addressed to me from my mother. The box contained a kaleidoscope. Pulling the brown paper off the box revealed a second layer of white paper, decorated with tiny stickers of hearts, butterflies, and daisies, and a poem that read:

The Kaleidoscope of Debbie's Life
I look into the viewfinder of
The kaleidoscope of my daughter's life...
In awe of the breathtaking beauty of
The sunlit colorful fragments,
Not wanting to miss a single facet.
With the slightest shift of the cylinder,
A fresh perspective delights my eye,
Yet another mysterious encounter along the path,
As she faithfully moves forward into the unknown,
With fear and trembling.
I reluctantly allow this beauty to recede from view,
As I turn the column cautiously,
Can this next vision be better than the last?
I eagerly await the next pattern of the glittering gems,
And gaze in amazing wonder.
As Debbie's life unfolds from

One priceless experience to another,
She knows that it is the Hand of God
Who prepares her steps and guides her heart,
In one continuous renewal of beauty and grace."
I am forever fascinated by
The kaleidoscope of your life!
Love, Mom

My perspective was altered by those words. I began to see my circumstances in a whole new light. And even though this poem was written and sent by my mother, I knew it was the heart of my Heavenly Father toward me. She could not have known the timing. God let me know that He had seen me, there in my loneliness, and was never going to leave me. He had a plan, a hope, and a future for me. The unmistakable hand of God was still on my life.

And, life did come together. I graduated with honors from NYU, got my daughter through high school and into college, moved back to my hometown, and met the love of my life. I also reconnected with my old church family and have made many new friends.

"You are unique and unstoppable." For the past two years, I have been hearing those words threaded through the Bible stories and challenging messages of some extraordinary women. Meeting weekly, we come together as sisters to make that heart connection with God in worship, and make those heart connections with one another. The Bible talks about this kind of bonding throughout the New Testament.

So often we do not realize our impact on each other. Recently, while at a planning meeting, I shared a passing moment in the hallway with one of these women. I told her I had been asking God for more boldness and that I believed it was coming. She looked surprised and said, "Really? You are one of the most courageous people I know!" and then turned and walked away. I was stunned, and I will never forget that moment. She doesn't even know that she spoke identity into me that day. I believed her.

I began to realize that all the experiences and challenges God allowed me to suffer, not only pressed me into a precious intimacy with Him, but were meant to be shared with others. So I rise now to tell my stories and encourage others to identify, value, and share their stories of God's faithfulness, because He is our hope in this life.

Another truth is that each one of us is not like anybody else. That makes life so interesting! Let's stop apologizing for who we are! Many women minimize and undervalue their experiences and triumphs. But believing, really believing that God wants to pour out all that He has poured in has been a gradual and deepening revelation to me.

I am so thankful for each person who has encouraged and ignited my faith through the years. We are to be there for each other, through word and deed. This is a powerful way God manifests His deep love for us.

I know God waits for me to wake up in the morning, just to hear my voice and help me along. He walks with me and patiently guides me, even when I am not aware of it. There is such power in the words we speak to each other. We each contain a kaleidoscope of stories of overcoming. *Your* unique story of faith has the power to change the course of someone else's life. Share it often and share it boldly!

Questions:

1. What life transitions have led you to invite Jesus into your heart?
2. During what transitions have you felt the most awkward and lonely in life?
3. During seasons of change, will you allow God to bring a whole new light to your circumstances?

Kimm Bryant - Limitless

"With men this is impossible, but with God all things are possible."

Matthew 19:26

Chapter 15

Limit - a point beyond which it is not possible to go.

Illness, disability and circumstances out of my control were parts of my life that limited me. I learned to live with and accept limits: I allowed them to define who I was, what I could become, what I deserved, what I could or couldn't do, and if God could ever use or love me. Early in life, I learned that limits can be set in place by others or I could establish them for myself.

Growing up I dealt with prejudice when we moved to Las Vegas in 1972. At that time, the town was still largely segregated, and we moved to the wrong side of town. I was either too dark or not dark enough; my hair was too nappy or too straight. My lips were big and my backside was too round. I was the short, skinny, redheaded, freckle-faced, little black girl that did not fit in with anyone. The white children were made to go inside when we rode our bikes down the street, and the black kids spit on me, pushed me and called me names like "Uncle Tom" and my favorite, "Oreo Cookie." They said I was black on the outside and white on the inside. I couldn't win with either group. Repeatedly, I heard, "She's cool, she is not like other black people," or "She thinks she's better than us because she is light-skinned." Most of my pre-teen and teenage years were spent trying to fit in, trying to be someone other than who I was.

When puberty hit, I developed a seizure disorder that stayed with me from about the age of 13 until sometime after I turned 45. For years, I was told there was nothing wrong with me based on the tests the doctors ran, yet I would pass out and have full grand-mal seizures. I was labeled a hypochondriac by doctors and peers. Finally, when I was 19, I had a seizure *in* the doctor's office and because they found no neurological abnormalities, I got a new label: "epileptic seizure disorder." Other than pumping me full of drugs, they didn't know what else to do for me. About a month later, I found out I was three months pregnant. They never ran a pregnancy test, so the baby was exposed to massive amounts of radiation and they rushed me to the hospital for an emergency abortion. They said the baby would not make it past six months, and that I was full of radiation poisoning coming from the baby.

About a year after the abortion, my seizures began to manifest differently. I developed a very severe intolerance for most foods, became allergic to insect bites and began to show signs of vertigo. I was the one that "always has something wrong with her." I was the hypochondriac. I heard this so much I tried to convince myself there was nothing wrong with me.

People would pray for me to be healed so I could live a *normal* life, at least by their standards. But I learned to live and function with physical, emotional and even addictive limitations. This was my normal. To think about living outside of what was familiar was scary. Because I had found a way to function inside the limits, healing would mean I'd have to face the addictions and emotional process I adopted to maintain my *normal* life.

My condition became my companion, my best friend. It was, for a season, the one thing that was constant, unconditional and familiar. This condition became my identity, even though it was painful, humiliating and uncomfortable. I knew that no matter how happy or sad it made me, how healthy or unhealthy I was, whether it was right or wrong…it was the one thing in my life that was always there.

At 35, I began what I call "reverse puberty," known as menopause, until I was about 45. At this point in my life, I started digging into the Word and developing my relationship with Jesus. It was comforting knowing I was able to serve Him right where I was. The smile I wore became an outward expression of the genuine joy and peace I called upon every single day. I obtained strength from the things Jesus spoke to me in our quite times together. He told me no good thing will be withheld from me (Psalm 84:11), I can do all things through Christ (Philippians 4:13), nothing is impossible with Christ (Matthew 19:26), and if I persevere I will receive the crown of life (James 1:12). Jesus became the One in my life who is always there.

During a church women's conference in 2012, we were asked to identify ourselves with one word that represented what God was trying to do in and through us; one word that described what makes me unique and unstoppable. My word was *limitless*; without limits, free from the things that hinder or stop me from becoming and doing all that my Heavenly Father has planned for me.

My body is now healed. There is a God who can do immeasurably above all I can ask or hope (Ephesians 3:14-20).

Questions:

1. What kind of limits do you have in your life?
2. Have you learned to live with and accept those limits?
3. Will you give them to God so He can set you free?

Sheila Sims - Answers & Acceptance from God

"Trust in the Lord with all your heart, and lean not on your own understanding. In all your ways acknowledge Him and He shall direct your paths."

Proverbs 3:5-6

Chapter 16

As a young woman, living in a growing metropolis, with abundant opportunities for career advancement, it seemed odd to question my life's path. But, I did anyway, wondering, "What else there could be to my life?" I was a community volunteer and active in local events and organizations, but I felt something was still missing. It wasn't the people, or the workplace or even the city causing this sense of dissatisfaction. It was a gnawing sense that there was more. Money and status were not filling that void.

Deep inside I had the seed of the gospel. I knew the stories of Christmas and Easter and could quote the Ten Commandments and the Lord's Prayer. I'd learned about the miracles of the Red Sea, the plagues, the ark, and the whale. The foundation of knowing God was there, and I never intended to stop pursuing God – it just happened. Like many adolescents, church lost its relevance for me and I didn't separate God from church. I began to notice behaviors in and outside of church: the outside church behavior didn't match inside church speech. I saw this over and over again, and so, attending a church became less important.

From time to time, I tried to return to the habit of going to church, but it didn't work out. I experienced rejection by some churches in my area: it didn't seem like they truly cared about people. Several churches I visited were not welcoming to college students. They were also not welcoming to me, as an African American. To me, it seemed that they wore "old religious hats."

Then one day, I reached out to God from the bottom of my heart, "God, make Yourself known to me – I cannot find You in church." He brought it all together for me: God brought a group to my city to start a new church. It was literally one block from my house, and my sister-in-law was involved so I already felt welcome. I connected there, re-established my walk with God and, with more understanding, accepted Jesus as my Savior.

Over the years, God has brought clarity about my past and He answered my deeply hidden "whys," when there was no one else to explain. Why did it appear that some children got more love than others? Why do adults use harsh words? Why would parents choose to be divorced and raise a child alone? Why did my mother have to die so young? I was 18. Why didn't she know she was sick? Why so much hurt and judgment among family members? I remember situations and circumstances that left their marks. Words of judgment left scars, and they made me feel less valued and inferior. In my secret place, God brought deliverance from the hurts that were tearing away at my self-esteem and keeping me angry and doubtful. During times of prayer, when I was first working through these questions, He brought understanding to me about who He is compared to what I experienced. He had always been there with me.

Throughout childhood and as a young adult, I was always looking for the approval of others. I pressed and pulled, cut away and glued on behaviors and facades to make myself match what the world said I should be. My aim was to have someone say, "We're pleased." Having the approval and validation from others was everything to me. It's been a process to undo self-destructive thinking and embrace my uniqueness. Now, I have victory over thoughts that kept me comparing myself to everyone and striving for man's approval. God revealed to me through His Word and through the Holy Spirit to strive to please *Him*, not people. His Spirit teaches me Jesus' compassion for people so that I will see what God sees in others and have His heart towards them. If someone requires something of me or is unhappy with me, I pray to understand their heart and love them in spite of what is said or done. Then, in love, I can respond without feeling the need to satisfy their unmet expectations.

I've learned to praise God for who He made me to be. There is no one else with my combination of experiences, education, preferences, dreams, passions, and relationship with God. I'm using all of them in His service as a teacher and worshipper and continue listening for His direction. I keep moving forward in my purpose even if circumstances or other people's opinions don't always match the plan. I am learning to walk by faith, not by sight, and not seek selfish goals but Kingdom purposes.

What I've come to understand that what I was missing in my life was having God in me – His love, His heart for people, His plan and purposes. I know now that I have a destiny in Christ and I'm continually learning about myself through Him. At every step, I seek

God to know *His* will and perfect plan. Whenever I'm faced with adversity or negative words, I know how to enter in to praise and worship so I hear and see clearly from God's Word. If I take a wrong turn and follow my own heart, I know to repent and seek God.

Along this journey, it's been a process of renewing my mind, placing my identity in Christ, heeding the call to spiritual maturity and having a positive impact on God's daughters. I'm unstoppable in my pursuit of God, His presence, His plan and His blessings!

Questions:

1. Have you ever struggled with separating going to church versus your personal relationship with God?
2. Have you ever experienced rejection in church?
3. Is it possible that what's been missing in your life, this whole time, has been having God *in* you?

Sharma Drake - Overcoming Addiction, Embracing Purpose

"I can do all things through Christ who gives me strength."

Philippians 4:13

Chapter 17

I am a believer in Jesus who is in recovery from drug addiction and codependency. Alcohol abuse, drugs, violence and adultery were normal in my family. During my childhood, my mother's mental illness caused very unpredictable behavior. She was often institutionalized for up to six months at a time. I lived in constant fear and pain, never knowing what to expect.

Because of my harsh environment, I retreated into fantasy and isolation, becoming very guarded and distrustful. At age thirteen, I took my first drink. Intoxication gave me immediate relief, but caused me to spiral into depression. Two years later, my soul felt hopeless and dark. I attempted suicide using my mother's psychotropic medications, causing temporary brain damage. Just like my mom, I was sent to a mental hospital, and upon my release, I was sent to live with my older sister in California for my sophomore year of high school. Being with her felt safe, but it was only a temporary situation, and returned home the summer before my junior year.

Shortly after my return, we learned that my only brother was killed in Vietnam. Life's pain became more than I could bear and kept piling on. I escaped into a dysfunctional relationship, became pregnant and married this abusive man as a result of pressure from my family. After my second child's birth, we separated. After his last release from prison, he committed suicide by heroin overdose.

By the time I was nineteen, I was alone, a single mother of two, an IV user of barbiturates, cocaine and amphetamines, and in enormous emotional pain. I felt hopeless and wanted to *die*. The drugs caused an abscess in my arm and I knew I needed medical help. I cried out to God sarcastically, "God if you want my life, You can have it, but *I'm* not moving! You will just have to come down from *Your* big heaven and get me!"

Shortly after, there was a knock at the door! I peeked through the blinds and saw Patsy, a Christian friend of the family. She said God had spoken to her in her thoughts to come to my house and see if I needed help. The Spirit of the Lord spoke to me at that time and said, "I work through those who believe in Me on earth to send and help people, so I sent Patsy to you. I *did* come from heaven through Patsy, so please do what she asks you to."

I showed Patsy my abscess, and she immediately took me to the hospital emergency room. The doctor said that I had blood poisoning and would have died within 24 hours. I was admitted, and Patsy's pastor came to the hospital and led me in a prayer to accept Jesus as my personal savior.

Because of God's intervention at age 22, I entered a Christian drug and alcohol treatment center where I learned more about Jesus, the Christian life and gained tools for recovery. I remained a resident of this treatment center for 13 months, and during that time my parents kept my two children. When I transitioned from inpatient treatment to the community, I took custody of my two children and began a new life; attending college full time, working part time and being a single mother.

After a while, I started isolating myself from my sober support systems, such as church, recovery meetings and more importantly, God. Life was busy, and I failed to prioritize what really mattered... my spiritual growth. As a result, I was lonely and depleted again. Instead of turning back to the Lord for restoration, or to church and recovery meetings for help, I defaulted into my old behavior to fill my inner void. This led me to an unhealthy and ungodly relationship with a man named Allen, a drug addict. Sadly, I relapsed. Then, Allen and I had a child together and ended up spiraling downward, hopelessly lost in the cycle of addictions. We began to pray to God for help.

God answered our prayer. I entered a treatment center called Conquest Center with my three children ages two, ten and twelve, and rededicated my life to my Lord Jesus. Allen's sentence for a robbery placed him in the same treatment center. That was the beginning of a new life for us and the children. I felt hopeful and loved by God and trusting that He would restore our lives.

I remained a resident of Conquest for three years and learned how to trust God. I served as a volunteer staff member and then as paid staff for a total of ten years. I ministered and counseled individuals who struggled with additions and related problems. I had the opportunity to share the good news of Jesus and the power of His great love and salvation, and then assist them in their recovery.

With God's help and guidance, I've accomplished many goals which may have previously seemed impossible, considering my past: goals such as obtaining my GED, getting a college degree with a 3.73 GPA, earning my Chemical Dependency License, and working as a Federal Case Manager and a Lead Chemical Dependency Counselor. More recently, I completed real estate school and have become a licensed realtor.

God had a plan for my life. I have heard it said, "God never wastes a hurt." God's favor has opened many doors for me to live a victorious and blessed life. In 2000, Allen and I were asked by the pastors at Capital Christian Center to start Celebrate Recovery, a Christ-Centered Recovery group. We have since been ordained as Pastors. Working through the recovery principals and steps has provided me with deeper insights into my own journey of recovery. Day by day, my soul is being renewed, restored and transformed into the image of my Lord Jesus. My recovery is a lifelong process. I've learned to be yielded to God's will and not my own, losing my self-centeredness so others benefit from my words and example. As a result, I've become a messenger of hope and healing for many who struggle with the bondage of addictions and compulsive behaviors.

Praise God for all He has done, all He is doing now and all He will do! Celebrating 31 years of marriage and 32 years of sobriety as a couple is a miracle. We also have an exciting ministry vision ahead. Our church is working towards building a faith-based residential recovery center called the "Whole Life Center" - a long-term residence facility for those who need a protected, healthy environment to learn how to live sober, productive lives.

Jesus is using my life as Luke 4:18 describes: "He has sent me to heal the brokenhearted, to preach deliverance to the captives and recovery of sight to the blind, to set at liberty those who are oppressed." To God be the glory!

Questions:

1. What pain from your past, could God use for His glory?
2. Where does your immediate relief from pain come from? Is it the from the Father's love, or from something else?
3. When the Lord sends a person to help you, will you allow them to help?

Peggy Barry - Created to Be Me

"The future splendor of this house will be greater than that of former times, and in this place I will give peace, declares the Lord Almighty."

2 Samuel 6:14

Chapter 18

March 28, 1945: The war was coming to an end in Europe, but my war was just beginning.

June 1944, two very young teenagers married at the ripe old age of sixteen. I was to arrive exactly nine months later. My father had to grow up fast. In order to support his young family, he enlisted in the Army. He was promptly sent overseas, and was gone for the first two years of this ill-fated union. The wait proved too much for my young mother. I was left in the care of her mother until my father returned. At the age of two, I was the casualty of a divorce. I was not to see my mother again for seven years. My nineteen year old father won custody of me. Suddenly he was given the task of finding a foster home for his little girl, as his next duty station was looming near. Finding a home for a toddler was not an easy task, especially a toddler with emotional issues.

God puts the solitary in families, and by His grace I was placed in the home of a very kind-hearted lady named Mary. She had never married and was the caregiver of her aging parents and brother. Maybe, just maybe, secretly I was the child she might have longed for. God knew, perfectly knew, she would be the one to shape me in those early years. He saw that it was to be the perfect match. She came highly recommended by the God who knew what all my needs would be. My father handed me over to her loving care. What wonderful years they were! I was the child she never had, and she, my missing mom. I was the object of her affection and very devoted to my care.

Despite all her duties and responsibilities to her parents, I was never in any way neglected. The greatest thing she imparted to me was a love for the Lord. We went to church every time the doors were opened and she was very faithful in teaching me about prayer and the Bible. I recall her showing me pictures of Jesus hanging on the cross. Sadness would settle over me as she would trace my little fingers over the cross and tell the story of His love for me. She was there my first day of school, and she was there to walk me home each day. "Jesus with skin on" was this lady named Mary. It was a happy time and it did not occur to me that I was missing a mother, or that this could all come to an end.

The day arrived when my secure little world ended, without any warning. There was a knock on the door and there stood my father home on leave. And at his side was a blonde lady with a child in tow. Was this my mom? Who was this lady? He was on his way to Korea and they were to marry. He was taking me to live with them. Still very young, Mary pleaded with him to let me stay until he was settled, but he won. I was heartbroken and shattered to leave the home and family who had sheltered me those early years.

I was on my way to parts unknown and it was all a blur. She and my father had not married before he left. Nevertheless, I was left in the care of this perfect stranger. The wait for my father was too long for her also. So, there was a wedding alright, but not to my dad.

What to do with "Joe's Kid?" was a conversation I overheard. The newlyweds did not include me in their plans. Now I was sent to live with the blonde lady's family. It was a nightmare. I was one of many kids running around. There were five of us in a bed. No discipline, no order, not enough food. The older kids bullied the younger ones. We were often left to our own devices and that was enough to scare anyone. It could have been a page out of Oliver Twist. I had been so sheltered, and now this.

Where was the Lord? Where was my dad? Or even the blonde lady with the kid? All those memories of Mary seemed distant and all innocence seemed lost. Disorder in the house was the call of the day. I missed a year of school. Seeds of discord began to take root in my heart. They would later bear fruit.

In the worst of times, I was rescued by my father's aunt. She found me! A perfect stranger had come to my rescue! And this one was also sent by God. The day she came to rescue me, I was wearing a pair of ratty jeans and my hair was matted and filthy. Even though I was finally leaving a bad situation, I kicked and screamed the whole time. The strangest thing had happened. I had bonded with these people! Kids will adapt to anything familiar. But God had once again stepped in and I was leaving Hell behind.

As my father's aunt took me under her wing, I went from little orphan Annie to Cinderella. But she dressed me from the inside out! New shoes, darling dresses, play clothes and toys! She was very old school and very religious. While she herself did not attend church, my cousin and I went faithfully. It was non-negotiable. She taught us to fear God, and I mean fear. She meant well, she had a deep religious faith, but not like the one I know now. She was a great mentor and taught us the importance of prayer, respect for the things of God and for others.

At an early age, I learned to give out of my allowance. She was big on helping the less fortunate. Mentoring was certainly her specialty. Keeping house, sewing, and cooking were also on her list. We were to be ladies at all times and she spoke frankly about purity. Encouraging us to always count blessings and give the Lord thanks for them all. She was from Old Mexico and knew poverty.

All too soon, my life with my aunt came to an abrupt end. My father, upon returning from Korea, found my mother and they remarried. I was nine. My aunt pleaded to let me stay, but it was not to be. They were my parents after all, but they were also strangers to me. Adjusting was hard. The seeds began to sprout. I felt displaced and very alone. My mom was expecting a baby. The bonding was reserved for the new life growing inside her. I acted out I'm sure out of desperation to be noticed.

The teen years were also difficult. We were a military family and had to move a lot, change schools and leave friends behind. My parents were not church-goers, but church was the only thing that kept me going. It was my escape. I would pray and talk to God. But still inside me there was a war going on.

Next, I married for all the wrong reasons. I longed for my own home and family, and longed for someone to love me and fill the void. As a result, I married someone I barely knew. I *just knew* the fantasy I envisioned would all fall into place: I would have the perfect man and kids, white picket fence and dog to match the dream. This was all to crumble.

It took me a while to understand that it was the Lord and His love that I really needed. Then, at age 29, the Lord found me...at a Billy Graham event. I went reluctantly at the invitation of a friend. You see, I had my own religion and I was very offended that she thought I was "lost." Yes, religion was all I had. There was no peace in my raging heart. On that day, the Lord took all that I had and changed my life. I walked down that aisle and said the prayer of salvation.

I wish I could say everything changed in that instant, but it took time for the Lord to untangle all the damage of those younger years. The gentleness of the Holy Spirit has come in His many forms to let me know that Jesus' love always brings healing and wholeness. His Word has been instrumental in replacing thoughts and attitudes I had learned as coping mechanisms. I found a Bible-believing church, got into a Bible study and into fellowship. The Lord even gave me a special mentor. Soon, I had a new prayer language, and I was telling others about the Lord. What a change!

The Lord has given me love, acceptance and hope. The more I read His Word, the better acquainted I become to the One who has given me this new life. I have found my true identity. I have come to understand this one thing more clearly:

I am created to be me, unique and unstoppable, not like anyone else, comfortable in my own skin, and designed for a purpose.

Questions:

1. Do you believe you were created for a purpose? What is that purpose?
2. Do you like you?
3. Will you allow God's Word to shape your life, from the inside out?

Colette Jensen – Strength & Courage Under Fire

"She is clothed with strength and dignity, and she laughs with no fear of the future. She opens her mouth with wisdom, and her tongue is the law of kindness. Charm is deceitful and beauty is passing, but a woman who fears the Lord, she shall be praised."

Proverbs 31:25-26, 30

Chapter 19

I never saw myself as a Proverbs 31 woman. All her virtuous qualities seemed far out of my reach. Then one day in prayer, as I shared this thought with God for the 100th time, the Holy Spirit stopped me in mid-sentence, "That's because you do not see yourself as GOD sees you; as He created you to be."

There are many times I have read scripture and somehow just didn't quite get it, or worse, I believed that truth was meant for everyone but me. Although there is no shame in not comprehending scripture, I want to *seek* to gain understanding. God's Word is the maintenance manual for life.

Growing up, I learned children should be seen and not heard. I was the oldest of three children; significantly older than my younger siblings and frequently became the stand-in mom when our mother was overwhelmed with life. At an early age, I learned to be very obedient and responsible. Those values serve me well now as an adult, but were burdensome as a child. I was the good, nice kid, who always did what she was told but wasn't ever encouraged to have an independent thought of my own.

I graduated high school at age 17. Soon after that, I ran headlong into the 60's revolution; the "me first" movement and the "whatever makes you feel good is okay" mindset. I was utterly unprepared for making life decisions, nor did I realize that unwise, emotion-based decisions come with lasting consequences.

For much of my adult life, I perfected my enabling skills. I held on to hurts and kept a record of wrongs. Life was unsatisfying and empty, and I didn't feel happy. I felt that my joy was held captive by all the wrongs others had done to me. There came a time when I had to stop blaming everyone around me for my failures and disappointments and take a good, hard look at myself. The world, and those around me, could not be changed. Even Gandhi said, "I must be the change I wish to see in the world." He was right!

There was a point in my 50's when I dedicated my life to God.

Each day, I would seek to draw closer to God and to understand the plan He had mapped out for me. But that did not mean my trials ceased. I found myself, yet again, in other difficult places; places I didn't volunteer for; places I arrived at because I missed the "danger ahead" signs. At 64 years old, I never envisioned my 30-year marriage broken and irretrievable, or my financial circumstances landing me at the bench of a bankruptcy court, or the job I had been in-training for, for seven years, being given to a complete stranger.

At this point, I had little courage left and zero strength to face these mountains. Inner-strength, I told myself, was not one of *my* personal strengths. I wore a mask that I allowed the world to see, but it wasn't the face in my mirror. I was broken and confused, yet not completely hopeless.

As I opened to Proverbs 31 again, I noted her strong character, great wisdom, valuable skills and compassion. I wanted these qualities, but in my own mind, I was sorely lacking. The Holy Spirit directed me to read the scripture again, and again, and again until, in His divine revelation, I settled on the last half of verse 30: "...but a woman, who fears The Lord, she will be praised."

The word "fear" in this context means reverence. It was new revelation, and I thought, "Why has it taken so long to see it from this perspective?" That gave me new hope, because I *do* reverence and honor God. God *could* still use me, despite the trials.

I will no longer be intimidated by the trials God allows me to face. Each one is a situation that invites me to trust my God and grow my faith. The more I trust God, the less I try to give Him helpful hints on how to fix difficult circumstances.

When you and I go through tough times, God will use challenging situations to teach us that we can trust Him. He supplies strength and power to His people to overcome every difficult day and disappointment. In Daniel, He reassures us, "Don't be afraid, for you are deeply loved by God. Be at peace, take heart and be strong."

We are courageous women, highly valued by the Lord!

Questions:

1. Do you see yourself as God sees you, as He created you to be, or do you have some other self-image that you see?
2. When you face trials, have you come to the place where you're no longer intimidated by them?
3. Have you had a challenging time in your life when you've completely put your trust in God? Has your heart learned that He is completely trustworthy?

Reva Brown - From Nothing to Everything

"The Lord is my light and salvation; whom shall I fear? The Lord is the strength of my life; of whom shall I be afraid?"

Psalm 27:1

Chapter 20

I spent most of my life making sure others received what they wanted or bailing them out of situations they put themselves in. I believed people would only like me or love me for what I could do for them. It became an obsession; an obsession that almost destroyed me.

When I was a little girl, I never felt a sense of belonging. I looked for ways to make people like me, to allow me to be part of their lives so I'd belong. I was the girl who sat by herself, quiet and passive, never being invited to join in with the others. My family seemed to consider and notice me the least. Maybe it was my very short hair, or the fact that I had the darkest skin color (I spent a lot of time outdoors), or because I was the shortest in stature. I was never given any type of compliment, no matter how hard I tried to make everything perfect. I was looked at with disdain, and reared with sternness and indifference. Sure, I had faults, but I always wondered what I could do to receive love.

On Easter, when I was 10 years old, I wore a beautiful pink flower dress, white shoes and white socks. My mother even allowed me to wear my hair down. "Oh my, she really loves me," I thought. Then darkness came again, and words of pain hit my heart. Imperfection became my burden that day, because, after all, my sister's hair was perfect. Mom just did not know how to "make me happy."

Apparently, I had been bad news from the time I was born, coming into the world all wrong, with my face covered with a transparent covering like ice that covers the pond during the winter months. I heard, "You look like a ghost." But, my sister was a beautiful baby, with her skin kissed lightly by the sun and her hair was filled with red highlights. All I ever heard was the imperfection of me and the perfection of my sister.

I thanked momma for making my dress. It was the prettiest dress I ever had. There is a place in scripture that says, "Honor your mother and father so your days may be long on the earth."

(Exodus 20:12) The Bible also says, "Parents, do not come down too hard on your children or you will crush their spirits." (Col. 3:21)

My spirit was crushed, and I hid to cry alone. I wondered if maybe my sister would look better in my dress. She looked like an angel in her white dress. It was silk, all shiny and smooth, with a white petticoat underneath. She would twirl and it looked like a large white rose. Momma would braid her hair the night before, and the next morning her hair would have beautiful waves. On this day, she wore a white bow in her hair. She was beautiful.

We all loaded into the 1957 Chevrolet daddy recently bought. Although it was almost two years old, it was like brand new to us. It was big - My sister, brother and I sat in the back seat, and there was still room enough for more! Our five-month-old, baby sister was up front in momma's lap. My other sister was no longer the baby, and her odd behavior started the day our new sister came home. My brother did not pay much attention to us. He was quieter than we were, and hardly said much at all. He was the most obedient child I know. In fact, I never saw my brother get in trouble.

As we drove to church, my sister whispered that she was prettier than me and momma gave me the ugly dress and she got the pretty dress. I did not like her much at that moment, because she was hurting me. Likely, there was some hurt in her too.

As I got older, my life in the family didn't really change. I continued to feel like the outcast. Sometimes, momma even called me a different name. So, I began looking for love elsewhere, in all the wrong places. I went to clubs, parties, and even to religious meetings, and still could not find the love I really needed. I ended up marrying someone who rejected me.

My life had been on a terrible roller coaster ride, and I was in such deep darkness that I couldn't see a future. I decided to commit suicide. My pain was all-consuming.

One night after my 12-hour shift at work, instead of going home, I began walking. It was late at night and snowing heavily, but I was numb with pain. I walked several miles and stopped in front of a church building. I walked toward it with eyes nearly swollen shut from crying. My world was falling apart. I screamed, "Where are You?" A couple minutes passed. And as I stood there, a small voice spoke so clear I began looking around to see who was there. The voice said, "I am not in that building. I am in you and you are strong, but you strayed from Me. Stop searching for what man cannot give you. Search for Me like you did when you were a child. "If my people which are called by My name shall humble themselves, and pray, and turn from their wicked ways, then will I hear from heaven and will forgive their sin and heal their land." (2 Chronicles 7:14)

God met me there, on that dark cold night, gave me some hope, and I did not end my life. Finally, the love I had been searching for all those years, found me. I have learned many things since that day. I've learned who I am and that I was never meant to fit into anyone else's mold. God made me unique. I am a daughter of my Heavenly Father who has loved me from the beginning of time.

Questions:

1. When have you felt like you don't belong?
2. Does your heart truly know that you belong to Jesus?
3. Will you give your heart to Jesus?

Margaret Stratham - Restored to Joy

"He gives them beauty for ashes and the oil of joy for mourning...that He may be glorified."

Isaiah 61:3

Chapter 21

My parents weren't supposed to have children. My older brother is adopted, and my parents were surprised when I arrived three years later, followed by another brother and two sisters. With generationally strong roots, Christianity was a lifestyle for my family, and both my parents modeled servant-hearted living. I had my first Holy Spirit encounter when I was eight years old; infusing me with a passion for teaching and ministering that is indescribable.

We lived in Tulsa. Although we had plenty of weak and faulty traits, I was blessed to be born into a supportive family who loved us and told us whatever we set our minds to do for God, we could accomplish it. That foundation would be important for me later in life, considering the many bumps and bruises that arose along the way.

My goals in life, deep down, always looked different than most little girls, and my experiences were different because of my family. We were all involved with my physically-handicapped brother and his terminally-ill classmates. My parents and others started the first physically-handicapped Boy Scout troop in the nation. I had the unique experience of being involved in the lives of children who would die before they were twenty. Around that time, my friend from church died. We were about thirteen years old. Her mother's outward grief continued for years.

My experience with loss and trauma at an early age created doubts in me about life, but these events also developed in me valuable tools when I began working with people experiencing trauma, grief and loss. I had to work through my own doubts, including questions like, "Was God a healer? Does He hear all prayers, including mine?" and I even questioned God's love toward me. I would later come to the understanding that my fears were unfounded.

Even though my goals and direction were quite different from my peers, I also questioned my identity during my teen years. I had a compliant personality and didn't want to stand out. "Peace at any cost" was my life, but it was a poor substitute for God's peace and joy, which I have come to love more than anything.

In college, my compliant side led me to make compromises at times. My Christian roommate got married, so I lost my strongest supporter. I was already finding it difficult to fit in at the church I was attending. I started dating a young Jewish man who filled my lonely Sunday mornings, because he attended church with me. By the end of our junior year, we made the difficult decision to break off the relationship because he didn't believe he needed Jesus as his savior. I was alone again.

About six months later, I began dating a guy from my hometown who seemed great on the surface, but had many dark secrets. One night, he drove up to my college town in the middle of the night, startling me, and the virginity that I treasured and was saving for marriage was stolen. It was replaced with a paralyzing traumatic event that would begin to feed fear, anger and the secret of being violated. In later years, by God's grace, compassion and understanding would flow out of me toward other women and girls in similar situations from the torment of that night.

I didn't fully deal with those hurts then, but moved forward in pursuit of my goals. I began fervently praying for just the right job, and in 1970 I accepted a job at the Navajo Reservation in Arizona. It was extremely remote. I had to drive over two hours just to do my laundry.

Once again, I would be confronted with choices and questions. My roommate, who was mad at God, didn't want to hear or talk about Jesus or anything spiritual. I complied. There were no churches for many miles either. My career started to take off, and I was making great secular, academic strides. My spiritual side, however, was waning. Jesus was advocating for me, and some miraculous events even occurred, but I made a very unwise decision when I married an unsaved man. We did attend a church faithfully that first year, but stopped after he was almost killed on the job and spent the next nine months in and out of the hospital. During that time he chose to quit taking his anti-alcohol abuse medication, developed some new "drinking friends" and became abusive. His bipolar personality raged out of control. I was determined to "love him enough" to make it work. I eventually discovered that I could not make him change or love me more. Then I had a very painful miscarriage before I even realized I was pregnant.

In 1977, God blessed me with a son, Aaron. Then my daughter Angela arrived in 1980. Unfortunately, the marriage had escalated into violence. I told God I was done trying to figure out how to fix anything in my marriage. I surrendered. Within a few weeks, we reconciled. God, in His wisdom, gave me another son, David, within the year. We moved to Colorado and my husband bought a business. I was beginning to gain strength spiritually, but the marriage didn't – it dissolved. The divorce took two years, during which time God healed all of the unforgiveness and anger that I had stored up for almost 15 years. Then, in one day, God provided me with a job back on the reservation. I had new direction, and life became more clear and fulfilling.

A second failed marriage to another man who walked away from God led me to a deeper understanding that Jesus Christ truly is more than enough for me, and is my provider for all spiritual, mental and physical things. Being a single mother had plenty of challenges, but God is a redeemer and used all of those negatives to show me His loving kindness and mercy. He even saved my son from death and two of my children from kidnappings.

In 2010, I took a giant step of faith, quit my job and moved to Washington to live near my children. He is truly a healer and restorer of all that the enemy has tried to take. I am blessed, I am safe, I am in relationship with great women of God and have the love of my family. God has continually sustained me and He has proved Himself faithful. The joy of the Lord is now my strength.

Questions:

1. When you're facing tragic circumstances in your life, who do you turn to?
2. When you have to make difficult choices, do you turn to God's Word and wise people?
3. In tough times, will you allow the Holy Spirit to guide you into truth?

Ruth Wade - Believe to Receive

"Surely he will never be shaken; the righteous will be in everlasting remembrance. He will not be afraid of evil tidings; his heart is steadfast, trusting in the Lord."

Psalm 112:6-7

Chapter 22

I was at work during a morning break... something I seldom do in the break room because there was always so much gossip going on there. That morning I went in, poured myself a cup of coffee and sat at a table by myself. Almost immediately, two of my co-workers asked if they could join me. It's always interesting, when you don't join in the grapevine talk, people don't really seek you out until they have a problem and need prayer or help.

The topic of conversation centered around one of the worker's health issues. The other lady had recommended a physician for her to consult, and they were discussing her diagnosis and whether she had been satisfied with the doctor. It seemed this particular doctor was hard to get an appointment with or maybe that she wasn't taking any new patients, I don't recall.

The Lord had been speaking to my heart about some medical problems I'd been experiencing. I had quieted those voices by saying, "When I have time, or, not right now Lord. We're in the middle of an audit, but as soon as I have more time...I will!" "I will, I will...just not right now!" I justified putting off what I really didn't want to do.

But on that morning, in that break room, it came not like that still quiet voice, but rather as a shout, a continuous roar in my ear...and it wouldn't release until it had my full attention. *Go see a doctor, go see this doctor, now.* I was trying to pay attention to the conversation going on around me, but it came again...*It's time, see this doctor NOW.* Then I was back in the conversation. I'd heard a doctor's name. What was it? Immediately, I asked what that doctor's name was again. They told me and reminded me she was not taking new patients, but that I could use their names as referrals if I thought it would help. I took the name, went to my office and called for an appointment. I shared that I had been referred by two co-workers whose names she recognized. Her receptionist set me up with an appointment to be seen in two days. Getting in so quickly was not typical with this physician.

That day I went to the appointment by myself, which never happened. My husband and I *always* accompanied each other on doctor visits.

At the office, the doctor greeted me and asked about my concerns. I explained my symptoms. She began to disclose what I felt were some personal, intimate details about herself. She spoke with a slight lisp and proceeded to explain it was the result of a cancer surgery. I recall thinking, why is this doctor disclosing these personal details about her health? As if she could read my mind she said, "I'm not sure why, but I felt the need to explain my lisp."

She performed the tests and wrote out a prescription for lab work at a clinic across the street from her office. My results would be back in a few days. She didn't foresee any serious problems and wrote me another prescription, this time for female hormones. Her receptionist would contact me with the results. I left feeling confused. I asked the Lord, why had the doctor felt the need to have this conversation about her health with me, a stranger?

I received a call from the receptionist, "Ruth, your tests are back. The doctor would like to discuss the results in her office as soon as possible. Can you come in today or tomorrow?" Those words "as soon as possible" engulfed me like a whirlwind fueled with questions. I scheduled an appointment for the next day.

The doctor entered the room. "Ruth, the news is not good. Your biopsy came back positive… you have cancer." I must have looked unphased by the results because she looked at me and said, "You don't seem surprised." I didn't know if she would understand, but I proceeded to explain. God had already been preparing my heart for the word I was about to hear. God had used this doctor's testimony to introduce me to the reality that cancer is no respecter of position or persons.

Was she a Christian? I don't think so, but God had used her nonetheless. I continued, "I'm a Christian, and the Lord spoke to my heart to explain why you had gone to such great lengths to explain your cancer. He used you as a buffer to cushion the words I would hear today. He prepared me through your testimony. I have to tell you though, doctor, this diagnosis does not line up with the words God has spoken for my life; to prosper me and give me health and a long life. All of my days were written in His book, not one of those days would be added to or subtracted. The Lord said be still and know that I am God. He is in control."

Did it scare me? Yes, but I chose to trust the Lord in this.

I researched the cancer so I would understand what I was up against, but I would not give it power. Who was I going to believe? The words I just heard? Death and a short life? Or what God had assured me, a long and full life?

I was referred to one of the world's best oncologists in Seattle. God provided me with the best, the very best, not only in the country, but in the world. Eighteen months and two surgeries later, there's no sign of the cancer.

I am smiling, serving God, and not quiet about it anymore. Psalm 112:7 says, "I will have no fears of news: my heart is steadfast, trusting in the Lord. My heart is secure, and I will have no fears." In the end, I will look in triumph on my foes. I am trusting God with all I have, all I say and all I do. Brave? No…Just trusting. God is good, all the time.

Questions:

1. What is your response when negative news comes your way?
2. Will you fully trust in God's Word no matter what news you receive?
3. Will you quote Psalm 112:7 and stand firm on His promises?

Dorothy Haase - A Foundation of Faith

"And His mercy is on those who fear Him from generation to generation."

Luke 1:50

Chapter 23

People know me as Aunt Dorothy. I was born during the Great Depression, in 1929, in Wisconsin. In 1935, toward the end of the Great Depression, my dad, mother, sister and I moved to Washington State looking for work.

During our first year in Washington, they picked fruit. Then my mother worked in a fruit cannery in Olympia until my brother was born. Dad started working for the Washington State Patrol and things picked up. A neighbor invited mother to go to a revival meeting in a nearby town where she gave her heart to the Lord, and so did I, at age six.

This began a journey for our family. My mother became a great woman of prayer and faith. I remember praying for my father to be saved and not go to hell. A six-year-old child's prayer is of complete faith, no doubt. Dad also gave his heart to the Lord.

Three women in our area began a prayer meeting: praying for a church to come to our community of Violet Prairie. So Violet Prairie Full Gospel Church was born and is still there today.

Our family grew even more: two more brothers and a sister. One day, my dad came home not feeling well. Mother was in Tacoma at a church meeting. By the time she came home, dad was really sick. The doctor came out to the house…said it was dad's heart.

This was the first time I saw a great healing miracle in my then twelve-year-old life. For three days people gathered and prayed. On the evening of the third day, dad got worse. My uncle Glen, dad's brother, went after the doctor. My dad whispered to a minister sitting by his bed, "Now is the time to pray."

Everyone began to seek God all over the house. All of a sudden, dad sat straight up in bed and began to speak in tongues. By the time the doctor got back, dad was sitting in the living room putting on his shoes and socks! God added forty more years to his life.

Both my parents served the Lord and all of us children went to church. I was thirteen when I received the baptism of the Holy Spirit. We all continued to serve in church. And, at home, we children knew that when mother began to pray, God answered. Coming home from school, we would hear her in her room praying. Dad always went to the barn. We lived on a seven-acre farm.

At 14, I suppose like many teens, I began to push the boundaries and cooled off in serving the Lord. Then God began to deal with my heart (mom prayed!), and I came close to Him again. I went to a revival meeting with my mother and sisters. After the preaching, my sister came back to me and pleaded with me to go to the altar. "But Sherrill I don't feel anything," but she kept on, so I went up. I said, "Lord, if this is You, then when I get up, let my brother Don be there." I got up. Don was there.

For the next year, I walked by faith. No feelings, just the Word of God and faith. Then He restored the *feeling* of His presence.

I also started teaching junior high Sunday school: found my niche! At 16, I met my future husband. He came to Washington after four years in the army. His family knew my family from Wisconsin, and my aunt introduced us. His name was Charles. We began to date, and in March, at age 17, we were married.

Things were not too good work-wise, so Charles enlisted in the Air Force in May 1947. We started out at McCord Field. While in the service, we always found a church to go to and take our children. We had two sons, and then a daughter. I started teaching junior high boys and girls again. We always made it our principle to live what we believed. So we prayed together, raised our family to know God was real and wanted to be active in our faith.

My sister-in-law became my mentor. She was so precious to me in my life, especially after my mother died. It was so important that I keep my relationship with the Lord Jesus fresh and vital, and not to let the cares of this life come in and steal away that sharp edge of expectation for what or where God was taking me next. Through prayer, God continues taking me from level to level in the knowledge of who He is and where He wants me to be in Him.

God has called *me* to pray – His part is to do the work. When God told me He was planting me and my family at our local church, I went up and told the pastor and his wife. Then when I went back and sat down, the Lord said, "Now you are responsible to pray for the ministry of this church," so I committed to doing that.

My one habit God had to break was a hard one. As the oldest of seven children, I always tried to find the answer when there was a need. God finally spoke to me one day and said, "Dorothy, you are trying to take My place. Only *I* can change people." He doesn't need me to be God in others' lives, but He will use me to help them if He needs to.

The outside shell of "Dorothy" is what God wants on the altar of surrender – then it's more of *Him* and the container is Dorothy. When that happens, I have learned to pray and lay the track so that God, the train, has something to run on. He's the strong One who does all we ask and pray. I get so much out of reading and studying God's Word and other books by great men and women of God.

I am so blessed. When my husband died, God promised to be my provider, healer and everything I needed. He didn't want me to put my faith and trust in anything else but Him. He spoke to my heart and said, "The place beside you is no longer empty because I have filled it with *My* presence." I've never been lonely. My life is full. He's given me extra grandchildren in my life, some daughters, great friends, and brothers and sisters.

God still speaks into my life daily, and I live in joyful expectation of what and where He is taking me next.

Questions:

1. Are you willing to live your life by faith versus feelings?
2. What commitment will you make to set aside time for studying, reading and growing in God's Word?
3. Will you live a life that surrenders *all* to Him and trusts Him in *every* stage of your life?

Alyssa Hamilton - Love Check

"And we know that all things work together for good to those who love God, to those who are the called according to His purpose."

Romans 8:28

Chapter 24

Let me take a second to recognize
that I realize that the disguise--
the mask I wear on my face--
to hide my once disgrace
is a misplaced gesture
birthed from things I let fester.

Things from my past
sneaking up as fast as lightning,
working as a spotlight brightening,
what I would hide under a facade.
You see, my family,
followers of the Most High God,
got some things wrong.

Standing in church, singing their songs,
pretending they belonged
as my parents were bound
and merely existing on rocky ground;
hoping no one found out
what Daddy-Number-One was all about.

Nearly in love, clearly in hate
they threw destiny to fate
and waited with bated breath
as their marriage faced its death.
Aborting their vows--their promises--
the mess we were left with was out of control.

The void was never full.
We were never whole.
It all simply faded into the nothingness
from which it came.
But all I knew was my empty stomach rumbling,
capsizing my thoughts, distracting me.
I just wanted to be free
from the poverty enveloping my family.

Developing a pain inside of me--
A burning, a churning--
a desire to tame Hunger
whom I called by first name.
Cold air was my blanket,
the sky my ceiling,
as we roamed
searching for a home.

Not surprising,
the family went through a little resizing,
as Daddy-Number-One kicked up his heels--
picked up and left.
He wasn't gone long
before Daddy-Number-Two came along.
Number One brought brokenness and neglect.

I suspect its effect
was a kind of self-preservation,
call it a kind of medication
for what I had to face
when Number Two took his place.
Like a lingering curse,
the second father was worse than the first.
The alcohol and the rage
were a tiger bursting from its cage--
claws latching onto the skin
and scratching places it shouldn't have been.

With biting and fighting
a tiger brings down its prey.

In the same way
he tortured me every day.
To Mom he pretended to care;
Behind her back he would stare--
a glare--
and declare that I was
worthless, disgusting, and like a disease.

I was a tease unable to please anyone.
I was the useless, ugly one.
I would cower in my bed,
His mantras repeated in my head
until I wished that he or I were dead.
At the age of nine--just a little girl--
I was introduced to the evils of this world.

After years I was relieved
when he was finally forced to leave.
Everything had faltered--
my dreams for life were altered.
No longer wanting to be a daughter or a wife,
Men were only torture and strife.
Not only did I fear men,
but mirrors were no longer my friend.

Unable to look at my own reflection,
trying to ignore the devastation--
the need for resuscitation--
that was me and my self-esteem.
My ugliness was all I'd see
when it was me looking back at me.
The words embedded in my brain
brought pain again and again.

You see, the history that was me
was one of world and self-hate.
Some tried to infiltrate the hate in me,
But it would only irritate
and infuriate me.

Encased in my walls of sarcasm and defense
I was always on the offense,
craving to restore my innocence.
I looked to my mom for answers,
but none came.
I turned to the media
and only saw emptiness of fame.
The Church who sided with Daddy-Number-One
and chalked other Daddy's actions to having fun
had already pushed me
to turn my heels and run.
And I was done with the Son.

It was years after, as I cried on the floor
that He came knocking at my heart's door.
At first it was subtle,
not wanting me to rebuttal
and rebuke Him;
He waited until I let Him in.
Immediately He had my trust,
I gave it freely because
His love was just love
not lust.

I wanted to readjust
My thoughts and what the church discussed.
On that floor, I find
that my mind was able to
traverse back in time--
before I knew Daddy-Number-Two's ways--
to the day I had rehearsed
a verse over and over again.
It said that God was
a God of great love not hate.

He didn't want to incapacitate me
or create a robot me.
He desired to navigate life beside me.
To fill the divide
between God and His bride

with arms open wide,
holding me in a tight embrace--
taking my shame away
and replacing it with grace;
opening the door to the secret place,
where the Father dwells.

He compelled me to rebel from the world
as He filled my every blood cell.
Instead of my hate song,
my living wrong,
I wanted to yell and shout
what true love was all about.
No longer the victim,
but now the victor
I let Jesus roar through my life.
Cutting away my anger with His spiritual knife.

He gave me the Bible--His very Word--
my sword and shield
and I yielded to His Spirit.
My mind was blown the day
when all that hurt melted away.
Praising God on His glory throne
I no longer wanted to postpone
the elation of my transformation.

Like rain giving to a flower
the hydration God poured onto me
as he cultivated my heart
let me know we would never be apart.
He reformed and redeemed me,
making it so I could clearly see
that He freely gave His life on a tree.
The ultimate sacrifice,
I was bought with a price
that needn't be repaid;
making the enemy's plans fail
as He tore the tabernacle's veil.

His love propelled Him
to wash away the sins of me and you,
and declared His love over daddies Number-One and Number-Two.
Through these new revelations
He changed my world view,
rearranged my self-view,
and gave me a new life-view.
Repeatedly God spoke over me,
convincing me to forgive, let go,
and live for Him.

At this point, it's fair to say,
I didn't want to just give my forgiveness away.
I had used my walls,
not intending them to ever fall.
my heart was recluse,
but I couldn't ignore His call.

Call it a reality check,
I call this a "love check"
when God broke the chains in me
And created a change of love in me.
I was no longer able to despise
the Daddies as I saw them through God's eyes--
the truth and not lies.
How could I hate them
when the One who loved me loved them?

I can't describe with paper and pen
the enormity of what can happen
when you live to forgive
others who have hurt you,
used you, abused you--
maybe even passed you around to their friends.

Nothing--not my past
that I've put on full blast
or the hate that casts a shadow--
Nothing compares to the love of the Father.
The love of my Beloved.

Questions:

1. As you do a love check in your heart and life, what chains need to be broken?
2. Who has hurt you that you need to forgive? Can you forgive them?
3. Will you allow the Lord to love you?

Salvation Prayer

If you've never prayed to God, asking Him for forgiveness of sins, and confessing that you believe Jesus His son died on the cross as payment for your sins, you can do so right now. Ask Jesus to become the Lord of your life. If you believe it in your heart, say this out loud (or your own version of it):

Jesus, I ask you to be Lord of my life, forgive me for all my wrongdoing. You know all my weaknesses. I ask you to surround me with great people who will lead and guide me, and I invite you to be the leader of my life. Amen

Now that you have said this prayer you are a part of God's family. The next step is to get plugged into a church family that teaches the Bible.

Contributors

Alyssa Hamilton is a full-time student and serves as youth worship leader. Her passion for poetry and fiction writing earned her an invitation and full scholarship to Oxford University.

Carla Baptiste is an Advocare Health and Wellness Advisor and serves on prayer team and worship team. She is married 26 years and has two grown children.

Christina Sipe is a business owner, physical therapist and serves in women's ministry. She is married 16 years and has three children.

Colette Jensen is a membership coordinator for a retiree organization serving 9,400 employees. She serves in women's ministry and has one daughter and four grandchildren.

Cortnei Boyd is a photographer and hosts, teaches and coordinates events in women's ministry. She is married three years.

Crystal Wade works in the human resources field, serves in women's ministry, student ministry and Twenty-Somethings at Capital Christian Center.

Danielle Payment is the women's pastor at Capital Christian Center, and served as youth pastor for 12 years. She is married 20 years and has four children.

Darci Coyne is a mentor and leader in the women's ministry, and teaches life classes in Celebrate Recovery. She is married eight years and has many spiritual children.

Deborah McLain is the writing director at Creative Force Press, serves in women's ministry and worship team. She is married two years and together they have three grown children.

Dorothy Haase served for 22 years as a Sunday school and Bible study teacher and now serves with intercessory prayer ministry. Married 59 years, she is widowed, with three children, nine grandchildren and four great grandchildren.

Kimm Bryant has worked in event management and currently serves the US Army in Casualty Assistance. She is married 24 years and has two children and six grandchildren.

Krista Dunk is an author, speaker, sign language interpreter, project director of Creative Force Press, and co-founder of Koinonia Business Women. She is married 20 years and has two children.

Margaret Stratham is a retired educator and serves in women's ministry, prayer team and Celebrate Recovery. She has three children, eight grandchildren and two great-grandchildren.

Melissa Wade is a State Auditor. She serves in women's ministry and on the prayer team, and has a passion for worship, travel and outreach. She has three grown children and one granddaughter.

Peggy Barry serves on the Prayer Team, hosts and teaches in women's ministry, and facilitates Prayer-n-Share with a senior group at a retirement facility. She is married 25 years and has five sons, 10 grandchildren, and one great granddaughter.

Reva Brown serves in women's ministry and sings in the choir. She has served in community outreach to the homeless and elderly. She has two children and five grandchildren.

Rhea Hernandez is a hairstylist, and serves with her husband as youth pastors and leaders of Formation student leadership training. She is married 10 years and has two boys.

Ruth Wade is a retired activities director. She serves in women's ministry and outreach to seniors. She is married 52 years and has three children, eight grandchildren, and nine great grandchildren.

Sharma Drake and her husband Alan are associate pastors. Together they lead the Celebrate Recovery group. Married 32 years, they have three children and three grandchildren.

Sheila Sims has a successful computer skills training company. She serves in women's ministry, worship team and children's ministry. She's been married 34 years, has one child, and fosters children.

Sherry Elliott served eight years in the Air Force. She volunteered in the children's ministry for five years before being ordained as the children's pastor in 2006. She is married 21 years with two sons.

Tammy Redmon is an author, motivating speaker, facilitator and coach. She's a teacher and host in women's ministry and teaches at Celebrate Recovery. She has two grown children.

Trisha Ferguson is a successful business owner and is the worship pastor at Capital Christian Center. She is married eight years, has one daughter and another on the way.

Valerie Avington serves in women's ministry and enjoys singing in the choir. She has been married 15 years and has four children.

Want to connect with us more?

Connect with us on Facebook by putting "*Unique and Unstoppable*" in your search box or by visiting www.UniqueAndUnstoppable.com!

"Unique & Unstoppable™" is a copyrighted ministry name for the women's ministry of Capital Christian Center (CCC), Olympia, Washington.

Visit Capital Christian Center's website at www.go2ccc.org.

Note: Scripture references in this book are from a variety of Bible translations.

To create a book like this for your ministry or organization, or to publish your own individual book, contact Creative Force Press today by visiting us on the web at:

www.CreativeForcePress.com

or

via email at **writeabook@creativeforcepress.com**

Creative Force Press
Guiding Aspiring Authors to Release Their Dream

Made in the USA
Charleston, SC
27 June 2014